FACING *the* SEDUCTION *of* SUCCESS

INSPIRING STORIES ON LEADING IN BUSINESS WHILE LIVING YOUR LIFE

JODI KATZ WITH JAN MICHELL

INDIE BOOKS
INTERNATIONAL

Base Beauty Creative Agency® is a registered trademark of JMK Creative LLC, dba Base Beauty Creative Agency

Where Brains Meet Beauty® is a registered trademark of JMK Creative LLC

ISBN-13: 978-1-957651-10-1
Library of Congress Control Number: 2022905681

Cover designed by Elisa Vitale
Interior layout designed by Bill Ramsey
Illustrations by Juliana O'Byrne

INDIE BOOKS INTERNATIONAL®, INC.
2424 VISTA WAY, SUITE 316
OCEANSIDE, CA 92054
www.indiebooksintl.com

To our guests, for generously sharing their stories of joy, struggle, self-doubt, perseverance—and success (often, all of the above)

To our listeners, who we hope will be inspired to share their own stories of joy, struggle, self-doubt, perseverance—and success (probably, all of the above)

CONTENTS

PREFACE

The stories presented here are from episodes of the podcast *Where Brains Meet Beauty*. The series began in January of 2017 and has continued with several new episodes launched each month, other than a COVID-19 hiatus in the spring of 2020. Titles and affiliations given are based on where each guest was at the time they recorded their episode. These are dynamic and ambitious people who may have moved on and up since they first stepped into the *Where Brains Meet Beauty* recording studio.

WORK, A LOVE/HATE STORY

Brains & Beauty-ism #1
Work hard. Then stop.

E ven if you love what you do—especially if you love what you do—it is easy to get sucked into feeding work's endless hunger. Work is infinite. Work is unforgiving. It is also exciting and joyful. And that's what makes it so seductive.

Not many books on leadership have the word *seduction* in their titles. It's a powerful word for me, crystalizing the dilemma that business leaders constantly face: how to embrace what we love about our work while keeping it from eclipsing the other parts of our lives. Whether you are a just-out-of-the-gate entrepreneur, a seasoned C-suite executive, or an employee of one of these leaders, you've learned that work is never satisfied. Work can take every moment, every thought, every ounce of energy you can give and still want more.

Success and seduction are not mutually exclusive, rather two sides of the same coin. We all want to be successful, whatever our endeavor. That desire is what leads to seduction. The challenge is to give ourselves fully to our work, which is necessary for success, without getting drained by work's immense neediness. That means knowing when to say, "enough for today," turn out the lights, and go home, physically and mentally.

This book offers insightful conversations on how beauty industry leaders strike that balance. Or valiantly try.

How I Got Here

The story of how I discovered work's voracious appetite starts early in my career. Those first years included an array of jobs—assistant to the editor-in-chief at *Cosmopolitan* and *Glamour* magazines, assistant account executive at advertising agency BBDO, copywriter at advertising agency Mezzina/Brown, plus gigs writing beauty copy for the Bliss and Avon catalogs, and other freelance work sprinkled in between. There was lots of uncertainty, some surprising layoffs, and a couple of painful and perplexing firings, along with remarkable learning, plus my share of rookie mistakes and the accompanying AFGOs (see Chapter Six). Between every job or gig, I would find temp work answering phones or filing, picking up little nuggets of business behavior with each assignment. I enjoyed working and took pride in my work, even when typing someone else's words.

My first full-time job in beauty was at L'Occitane en Provence, where I was hired as the France-based company's first and only copywriter in the United States. At that time, the company still had an entrepreneurial feel, and there were needs and opportunities everywhere, which I embraced. They trained me in fragrance, skincare, and formula development, and sent me to meet the beekeepers, olive growers, and lavender farmers who supplied key ingredients. I volunteered for extra projects, boldly leaning in and finding that my opinions were valued. I was a sponge, absorbing everything, learning art direction and production, and gradually evolving into the creative director for the US. I worked hard and loved it. And I found my professional voice.

By my fourth year at L'Occitane, I began to get itchy. I adored the job, but it was no longer stretching me creatively. Plus, I felt ready for the next part of my life to begin. I was married and thinking about starting a family. I considered the length and intensity of each workday, my commute, and how drained I felt each night when I got home. I simply did not see parenting fitting into that schedule. I also realized that I had grown into a respected creative director and was confident I could apply this experience elsewhere in an environment that was more flexible and forgiving.

Near the end of my tenure at L'Occitane, I had been taking on side projects as a copywriter and creative director, so I was constantly working, day and night. As I was pondering my next step, I realized that my side hustle had grown to the point that it could become my main hustle and support me. I wasn't sure how I would structure this new direction, whether I would continue as an independent freelancer or form a creative entity. Still, I knew I was ready to be the one making those decisions. I took a deep breath, gulped, and resigned.

Moving Right Along

After taking that plunge, it became clear to me pretty quickly that I wanted a structure within which to work. I had some steady freelance clients, and they became the foundation upon which I started my agency, now called Base Beauty Creative Agency (BBCA), celebrating our fifteenth birthday. It has been a slow but steady build. The hustle is still constant, but now I have a fabulous team to hustle alongside me. Even after fifteen years, there are ups and downs, moments when things are humming along and moments when I'm biting my nails with worry. COVID-19 provided plenty of those oh-my-gosh-can-we-survive sleepless nights, as it did for everyone in the beauty industry and many other industries as well.

One of the boldest steps I took was positioning the agency as a specialist in the beauty and wellness space. People said I was crazy to do that. People told me that I had ideas and experience and a talented team that could provide creative direction for anything, from auto parts to computers to widgets, and that I should not limit the work available to us. But I didn't listen. My passion and my experience—as well as the passion and experience of those working with me—are in beauty, and I believed then, as I do now, that there is value in being a specialist. We know the industry inside and out. That deep industry knowledge helps us differentiate the merely interesting clients from the game-changing ones. We call on our expertise to determine which clients are the best fit for us and how we can help them stand out from their competition. Although there have been some lean times when I could have used an auto parts client, my decision to focus on beauty has been borne out.

There's another reason specializing has been the right road for Base Beauty. I believe in what the beauty and wellness industries provide, which is much more than the newest shade of lipstick. The products we create and market help people look their best, which helps them feel their best. They solve problems, sometimes agonizing ones, that are often front and center on the face for the whole world to see. They can also heal from within, contributing to feeling healthy, energetic, and confident, and liking what you see when you look in the mirror. Their impact on self-esteem is enormous. When anyone says the beauty industry is just fluff and vanity, I jump right in to defend it, especially our work at Base Beauty, where we take a fresher approach to beauty. We emphasize transparency. We celebrate the consumer's diversity and uniqueness. We encourage our clients to avoid retouching. Top of mind in all we do is helping customers to feel empowered and included, not alienated, by beauty marketing. We see such efforts elsewhere in the industry. There is substance here.

Perhaps because of all the benefits the beauty and wellness industries offer, they attract amazingly open and principled folks who believe deeply in the value of the products and services they provide. I can't know for sure, but it seems that there is a disproportionately high level of philanthropy and generosity within the beauty world, whether it's donating products to homeless shelters, mentoring the next generation of leaders, or sharing survival tactics during the pandemic. I am honored to be part of this big-hearted community.

The Not-So-Secret Society Of Those Who Overwork

As Base Beauty grew and I met more and more industry peers, I observed how people work. I often saw people working grueling hours, sometimes to the point of burnout, even life-threatening burnout. I noticed that some people wore their endless work schedules and high stress levels as a crazy badge of honor that showed how dedicated they were to their work. I have always understood the drive to work like that. It's especially common among entrepreneurs who give birth to their baby businesses and nurture them with care, wearing every hat when they can't afford to hire help. That level of devotion is fine for some—I am not judging anyone—but it was not what I wanted from my professional life.

Of course, there were times when I was guilty of the kind of overwork I saw in others. The more headway I made with Base Beauty, the more conflicted I became. It was exciting to see what I was building, so logic would dictate that if I worked harder, longer, more intensely, I would grow the business faster and feel great about all that progress. There I was, caught between seduction and success. I knew one thing for sure: I did not want to work as obsessively as many of my industry colleagues, whether corporate executives or entrepreneurs. After all, having time for a life outside of work had been my main reason for starting the agency in the first place. But there were long stretches—years, in fact—when the stressful side of seduction had taken over.

What I didn't know back then is that that the temptation to work incessantly is an identifiable phenomenon and a common one. It's a type of addiction, each step on the path to success beckoning us, compelling us, almost daring us to resist taking the next one and the next. All around me, I saw people being pulled in this way and how it could happen to me.

The Birth Of A Podcast

Fascinated by the dichotomy between the goal of success and the pursuit of success, I wanted to explore it further. That's why, five years ago, I started our podcast, *Where Brains Meet Beauty*. Insanely curious about everyone's story, I saw the podcast as a way to dig deeper and learn more about my peers than I could by quickly asking about their kids or their last job while rushing into a meeting or during chitchat at industry cocktail parties. The target is the intersection of professional desires and personal backstories. I don't need to hear about product launches or upcoming marketing campaigns in this forum—there are plenty of other ways I stay current on all of that. I want to learn about my guests' childhood dreams, their motivations and goals, and how they feel about their journey so far.

Our conversations are precisely that, one-on-one explorations of thorny and not-so-thorny topics from both participants. My aim has been to humanize our industry by creating an intimate and safe space in which sharing is encouraged. I frame my questions with empathy, helping guests feel as if they are talking to a friend, albeit a friend who has experienced some of the same professional speed bumps as they have, which adds an extra level of connection. The mood is relaxed and easy, with humor and drama in equal measure. Every recording session has been a pleasure for me.

While I approached the podcast hoping each episode would be revealing, I was not prepared for how deeply soul-baring they have turned out to be. Episode after episode, I have been blown away by how open and honest my guests are with me—and how that has allowed me to open up in the same way. Recordings have turned into quasi-therapy sessions all around. As I was planning my approach, I realized that when business leaders are interviewed, they are typically asked about their products, their market share, their growth potential, and their acquisition strategies, but rarely about themselves and the meaning they find in their careers. *Where Brains Meets Beauty* provides a much-needed service to my guests, a chance for them to vent anything they need to vent. I steer the discussions toward the personal, and guests know that coming in. The sessions also provide a crucial outlet for my own feelings, fears, and challenges. I did not walk into this entrepreneurial life with a toolbox for finding either sanity or serenity, but our conversations have helped me find some of both.

As the series has continued and we have archived more and more episodes, I have seen recurring themes and emerging patterns. A number of guests have spoken of a personal challenge as the catalyst for their business—a parent's death that dashed a childhood dream, or an unexpected job loss that allowed an idea to percolate. Many have shared stories of setbacks and missteps, eager to unburden themselves with someone who knows the industry but is outside of their company. Almost every guest has talked about the struggle to maintain some sort of personal life while growing a business or career—a topic reflected in the title. Seeing these commonalities, I decided there was value in bringing them together. This book is not just for the beauty and wellness communities; these challenges are universal. Sharing them lightens the load.

My Aha Moment

Two years ago, after about one hundred podcast episodes, and in the pre-pandemic era, I had an epiphany. Base Beauty was burgeoning with great clients and an amazing team. I felt joy in my work, pride in our growth, and challenged creatively. Who wouldn't want more of the same? I definitely felt the seductive pull to work more and more. But I continued to grapple with the temptation. I could put in the hours. My children were older and more independent. They would understand and respect their mom's dedication to her business. My forty-something muscles would try to hold their own until I had more time for them at the gym. But what would I be giving up in order to spend more hours on my computer?

An image popped into my head. I saw myself sitting on the proverbial fence. On one side of the fence was the work I loved. On the other side of the fence was everything else I loved— my kids, my husband, my workouts, my garden, my travel, my books. What I realized is that I had been thinking of the balancing act in absolute terms, terrified that if I leaned into one side of the fence, everything on the other side would be ignored and forgotten. Now I saw that I could spend time on one side, then jump to the other side, and keep going back and forth. It didn't have to be one side to the exclusion of the other. It might not be perfectly balanced, but it can work (see Chapter Three). What had gotten in my way was seeing so many people around me who spent all their time on one side of the fence, by choice or not. My fence vision was a revelation, and these last two years have been ones of sweet satisfaction and diminished stress, pandemic and all.

If you follow our podcast, you might notice a slight change in the tone of these post-epiphany conversations as I share my evolution with my guests. I'm certainly more relaxed, but I also realize, more profoundly than before, that everyone has to find their own way of filling the buckets of their lives. I no longer react viscerally when I hear of someone working themselves to the point of exhaustion, even though it saddens me. As you read through the stories that follow, you'll see that these beauty and wellness leaders are defining how they want to work and how they want to live, facing the challenges with guts, grit, and grace. I think you'll be moved, as I am every time I step into our (now virtual) recording booth.

In our office, we have a bell that we ring when good things happen. We focus on gratitude and celebrate wins of every size, from major victories to tiny triumphs—signing a new client, welcoming a new hire, times when work is well received, or our artful responses when work is not well received. We do this to remind ourselves what we love about our work, to keep the negative stuff from dragging us down, to support each other, and to keep finding the fun. Working remotely during COVID-19, we sent every team member a bell to ring on their own or during Zoom meetings when we all ring them together, creating a delightful cacophony.

Thank you to every guest who has shared their story. They have made me more grateful than ever to be part of this remarkable community of bold, thoughtful, kind souls who do their best every day to move the ball forward for themselves and their colleagues in honest and authentic ways. In an industry centered on making colors and creams and lotions and potions, it is a joy to present our own kind of truth serum.

Ring the bell. ❖

2

FIRST STEPS ON THE LONG AND WINDING ROAD

Each step gets you closer to . . . somewhere

There's a question I ask each *Where Brains Meet Beauty* guest that's at the heart of why I started the podcast in the first place: How did you get here from there? Wherever their "there" happened to be, the answers have been as varied and fascinating as the guests and always launched lively, complicated, often poignant discussions. Few guests had a childhood dream of working in the beauty industry. Hardly anyone's path has been a straight line. Every story is riveting.

While therapy is not our intent at *Where Brains Meet Beauty*, there is comfort in sharing one's en route challenges, the inevitable pitfalls, the rookie mistakes, the forks in the road, and the sticky decisions that ensued. It's helpful to vent about the endless hours, the self-doubts, and the stress that come from reaching higher and further, from wanting something more or something else. Guests often express appreciation for the opportunity to open up about the personal side of their professional journey in a safe space with someone who has been there, too.

The bumper-sticker takeaway from the stories that follow is obvious: You never know where your path will lead, so don't panic if where you are at the moment is not your goal. You never stay in one place for long. ❖

> *"There is something to be said for triumph through challenge."*
>
> —Soyoung Kang
> Chief marketing officer, eos Products
> (Episode 180)

From the age of eleven, Soyoung wanted to be an architect. She saw it as a perfect marriage of art and design, which she loved, and math and science, which she also loved. She first learned about the field of architecture from watching reruns of *The Brady Bunch*—Mr. Brady was an architect, and she thought that was pretty cool. She set her sights and mapped her course. But life had other plans.

From an immigrant family, and the oldest child who spoke English fluently, Soyoung remembers, "There was a lot of responsibility that fell on my shoulders from a very young age, helping my parents out with their business . . . helping them navigate things like picking an HMO plan for our health insurance for our entire family. These are things that are really formative for a young person and really teach you to be reliable, accountable, responsible." Then, as she was finishing her undergrad studies in architecture at MIT, her father died suddenly. She knew she needed to become financially independent as soon as possible, and architecture, with its advanced study requirements and apprenticeships, was a career with a long, slow build. Returning from a one-year Fulbright

Fellowship to study architectural theory and history in Korea, she needed to find a real job.

What she found was a position in management consulting at Kearney. After fitting in business school at Wharton, she was hired by Boston Consulting Group, an opportunity she describes as a gift, since beyond a paycheck, it helped her develop the leadership skills that are vital to her work today. At BCG, she worked with client Bath & Body Works, her first experience with the beauty biz, and discovered she loved it. When Bath & Body Works hired her, she was on her way to the beauty C-suite. She remarks on how valuable those first jobs have been: "What I actually got out of my work in management consulting, which in varying ways spans the first decade of my career, was a way of looking at everything that I do today, thinking about things strategically, in structured ways, applying big picture frameworks, thinking about things from thirty thousand feet before I zoomed down to the details."

Perhaps because of the adult responsibilities she had borne as a child, when life took that tragic turn, Soyoung faced the disappointment head-on and regrouped without whining or complaining. She never thought she would find another passion after her architectural dreams were dashed, but she did. Hers is a story that exemplifies the theme of "you never know." ❖

"I see my acne as a blessing.
It gave me a purpose in life."

—Cassandra Bankson
Online beauty pioneer, influencer
(Episode 54)

Growing up is hard enough, but for Cassandra Bankson, an extreme case of cystic acne covering 90 percent of her face made it a lot harder. While others were forming friendships and developing social skills, she was taunted and bullied, spending her formative years in a harsh, lonely world. Outside of school, her afternoons were spent cycling through endless doctors' appointments and medications in what would prove to be a futile attempt at a cure. No one seemed to be able to help her. Acne ruled her life.

Interestingly, it was Cassandra who found the solution, pondering whether her diet and stress might be among the causes. When she posed her theory, the doctors just handed her more pills and creams. So in true entrepreneurial fashion, she started researching foods that affect the skin and the emotional component of skin conditions. She came up with a diet and stress-reducing regimen that helped her heal, eventually leading to the clear, beautiful skin she has today. She reflects, "I recognize that if it weren't for all of that trauma I've been through, I never would have started speaking about acne. I never would have gone to school to try to study skin. I never would have gotten clear skin, which I have now, because I worked hard at it."

Two meaningful outcomes evolved from Cassandra's painful childhood and journey to healing. Disappointed by so many dismissive dermatologists over the years, particularly by their lack of sensitivity to what it meant for a young girl to live with cystic acne, she decided to go to medical school. She plans to be a different kind of dermatologist, with a holistic approach that encompasses nutrition, emotional learning, and social components, along with traditional medicine—an approach she is developing on her own since it's definitely not taught in medical school.

On her way to becoming the type of dermatologist she believes the world needs, Cassandra decided to share her story, creating a YouTube video that has over a million subscribers, many of them teens and young women going through the heartbreak she experienced. Cassandra continues to be incredibly moved as others struggling with acne express their appreciation for one authentic, understanding voice where there had been none. As she observes, "Now I realize that I have such a bigger purpose, and that I'm able to connect with people, with my followers . . . . I believe I'm making a difference in the world, and there's no better feeling than that." ❖

*"I remember all the challenges I had . . .
I was terrified every day."*

—Karissa Bodnar
Founder and CEO, Thrive Causemetics
(Episode 151)

Everyone experiences loss at some point. It's the way you handle it that defines character. Some curl up in a corner. Some use it as a catalyst for the next chapter. When Karissa Bodnar's twenty-three-year-old best friend died of cancer, Karissa did the latter. She was working in product development at L'Oreal. Inspired by her friend's compassionate and vivacious spirit, and the meaning she had infused into a short life devoted to public service, Karissa knew she wanted to find her own way of giving back. She also had a dream of developing a line of vegan beauty products. So she decided to start a business that combined the two goals. In Karissa's words, "When my friend was gone . . . it was one of those moments for me where I really thought about what my purpose was because she knew her purpose. While I was climbing the corporate ladder, she was teaching English to orphans around the world. I knew that I wanted to be giving back. And I also wanted to create amazing products. I couldn't work for a brand like that because it didn't exist. That's really where the idea for Thrive Causemetics was born."

Many companies implement philanthropic programs only after they have achieved a level of success. Not Thrive. From the day the company opened its doors, it has followed a model of giving back that is built into its core mission and structure—and even its name. For every product Thrive sells, it donates another to causes that support and empower women, from women vets to women in homeless shelters to women battling cancer. Since its inception, it has supported more than fifty organizations and made donations worth many millions.

There's a lot that's impressive about Karissa, from the resourcefulness with which she taught herself formulations—as a child, she melted her sister's crayons, along with mashed-up petals from her mother's garden, to make lipstick—to the way she started Thrive at her kitchen table with her savings, to dealing with sexism and ageism (the twenty-something CEO was often mistaken for the intern). Thrive and its still-youthful founder exemplify what can be done when you create a business around a heartfelt policy of giving back, and an environment in which everyone can thrive. ❖

> *"It's the difficult times in life where*
> *we learn the most."*
>
> —Suzanne Somers
> Actress, author, founder of Suzanne Organics
> (Episode 178)

Suzanne Somers is light years away from the ditzy character she played on the hit sitcom *Three's Company,* which ran in the late seventies and early eighties. (That's why they call it acting.) In fact, she is a bestselling author, a talented entrepreneur, and an important voice for wellness and holistic healing.

Coming from a challenging childhood where she often had to hide from a violently alcoholic father, she somehow developed a remarkably optimistic approach to pretty much everything—so much so that her family nicknamed her Rosy. She attributes her lemonade-from-lemons attitude to this toxic home environment, surviving by fantasizing about her future success, picturing herself on stage making her family proud, which of course she eventually did. No wonder she believes that childhood dreams can be very potent. As she puts it, "I just keep moving forward. When I go through a difficult period, I always sit back and think, 'What am I trying to teach myself this time?' It helps me in not ever getting down."

When it was time to pivot away from performing, she immersed herself in the study of holistic wellness, taking deep dives into how supplements and organic ingredients work on the cellular level. While not a doctor, she has studied hard and learned a lot, using her celebrity to gain access to the best experts and pick their brains. This has enabled her to become a respected spokesperson on the topic of holistic healing, fighting through the many misconceptions out there. Along the way, she founded Suzanne Organics, a line of organic skincare and supplements.

Perhaps her most remarkable talent is her ability to extract digestible takeaways from confusing, dense, and data-filled information on holistic healing, clearly explaining and interpreting the experts' jargon for her followers. "I can take boring doctor speak—they're fascinating people, but they don't know how to explain things—and decipher it so that I can understand it and have my aha moment. Then I know everyone else will understand it, too." The irony is not lost on her that, having played one of the dumbest women on television, this smart, upbeat survivor is now dumbing down wellness to make it accessible to millions—an irony she celebrates. ❖

"Girls were missing school.
We thought that was crazy."
—Elise Joy
Executive director, Girls Helping Girls. Period.
(Episode 123)

When Elise Joy was blindsided by a mean-spirited layoff from her job as a news producer at a major network, she decided to make something positive come of it. That something arrived via her two teenage daughters. As the family volunteered at a local food pantry, they were shocked to learn that food stamps could not be used for personal hygiene products. The girls put two and two together and realized that they had classmates—right in their middle-class community—who were missing school a few days each month because they couldn't afford the supplies they needed. And their educations and self-esteem were suffering because of it. The Joy girls asked their mother to help them find a solution.

Elise describes the early evolution: "We just started collecting products to donate to the food pantry. It was so well received that we asked some friends to help, and within a couple of months we had fifty thousand products in our house. . . . After we gave away all those products, we just said, 'We can't not keep doing this.' It made such a difference to the people we helped, because we did our best to give a year's supply. The families we gave them to were so touched. It took a huge problem off their plate for a whole year."

Eventually, this powerful mother-daughter trio started a nonprofit to support the fight for menstrual equity. It started slowly, but it grew pretty quickly as the Joy family grasped the enormity of the need and the simplicity of the solution. Girls Helping Girls. Period. collects and distributes personal hygiene products through schools, universities, food pantries, and other community organizations, where they are available to girls who have been missing classes or feeling stressed out at school during their periods because they couldn't afford the supplies they needed. The foundation has expanded its outreach by building a network of sponsors, partners, and donors, and a board of accomplished professionals. Along the way, the three founders have learned about the bigger issue: systemic economic discrimination against women and girls.

Elise has brought all of her high-level producer skills to the foundation, but does not miss the high pressure and long hours of news production. She does admit that it took a while for her to break some habits, and her family had to keep reminding her not to "produce" everything. She finally has learned about working at a saner pace: "One of those things that I'm trying to focus on now is just taking a breath. So you don't get there on time. So it doesn't all look perfect. It turns out, it's just fine. It's actually sometimes a lot nicer."

If you had asked Elise what she would be doing in five years when she was working in the intense world of network news, she would not have come close to describing this path. The fact that the motivation came from her daughters makes their simple yet vital work all the more meaningful. Theirs is a moving story of seeing a need and stepping up to meet it, powered by two caring teens and their equally caring mom. ❖

"Just go for it, so you don't have any regrets."

—Deborah Lippmann
Celebrity manicurist and founder, Deborah Lippmann
(Episode 146)

When it comes to teetering on the edge of your dream and pondering whether to take the plunge, sometimes you need a gentle nudge, sometimes a kick in the butt. Deborah Lippmann's passion was music. But needing to support herself while she was getting her singing career going, she went to cosmetology school to study manicuring, glad to have a skill where she could sit down all day since she was on her feet singing in clubs at night. It turned out that she really liked this side hustle, and she was also really good at it, developing insights into how women feel about their hands, and observing a general lack of knowledge about hand and nail care. Working in a fancy salon in New York, her ideas on better nail care were percolating. Bobby Brown became a regular client and started to give her that gentle nudge. But it was a good friend who gave her the kick in the butt that resulted in her two loves—music and nails—switching places in importance.

While growing her roster of celebrity clients, this former nail biter started a line of polishes and nail care products from scratch. Not having a clue how to create a product, package a product, market a product, or run a business, the learning curve was massive, but so was her commitment. Like most first-time entrepreneurs, she was, at times, overwhelmed by the challenges but equally glad for the opportunities to learn something every day. Her sage advice for anyone considering starting their entre-preneurial adventure is to go for it. "If you believe it, you can do it, you can find a way to make it happen. If you have a dream, you should not do what I did, and have to have your friend finally look at you and say, 'Do it, or shut up about it.' If you just do it, then you'll have peace of mind."

Happily, as she works with her star clients and markets her nail care line, she is able to continue her performing and recording, sleep being overrated in her world. Deborah's is a truly integrated life, with polish colors named after song titles, and manicure clients who come to hear her sing. She is forever grateful to the friend who gave her the fateful kick that launched it all, and thrilled that her main hustle and her side hustle now work hand in hand. ❖

MY ROAD

I was on a jagged journey early in my career, back and forth between advertising and publishing, with stops for temp gigs in between, before my first "real" job in beauty at L'Occitane en Provence. This jumping around was unexpected. In college, I had assumed that I would find a role or a field, set my sights on a goal, and proceed in a straight line through that industry. The engineering majors around me had such plans, and it seemed that most of my other classmates did, too. But once I began that first advertising job, I realized that I did not fit into that super-planned world. Unlike my colleagues, I was not obsessed with which brands switched agencies or who had landed a fat new account. I was disappointed, and frankly, a little lost. The phrase that kept reverberating in my head was, "These are not my people."

It wasn't until a few jobs down the road, when I was working for a seat-of-the-pants startup website, that the light bulb went on that said, "You don't have to do it in a straight line. You can zig and zag and change your goals, or change your industry, or change anything." This startup was iffy, edgy, a little chaotic, and a lot underfunded, with all kinds of twists and turns. By that point, I was able to look back and appreciate the skills I had acquired at each job, even the jobs I hated. I realized I did not have to fit into a mold. I didn't even need to acknowledge that there was a mold.

Years later, I remember speaking with a woman at a cocktail party. We were talking about careers and goals. She was a physician and was talking about feeling trapped because she really didn't want to be a doctor anymore. She had made that decision when she was eighteen, and now she was in her mid-fifties. I asked her, "Why do you still have to be a doctor?" She answered, "Because that's what I am." When I suggested that it was OK to change her mind, she was stunned. It had never occurred to her that she could do something else. It was a short but memorable conversation about the decisions we make, when we make them, and the possibilities that exist when we choose to change course, even though it's not easy. ❖

Lesson Learned

We all start with an empty backpack and fill it with skills and experiences as we go and grow. I finally learned to keep my backpack open and believe that everything I put into it would eventually be valuable—maybe in a quirky or surprising way, but valuable just the same. The zigzagging road is still a road to somewhere. ❖

SOUND BITES

Share your story.

Trust your gut.

Don't whine.

Make lemonade.

Look around you.

Be grateful.

Give back.

FOOD FOR THOUGHT

➤ Have you found your people? Are you fortunate enough to be working with them?

➤ Have you ever felt stuck? Have you hesitated to change course because it would seem as if you were admitting defeat, or it just seemed too hard?

➤ Can you think of skills and experiences you acquired in previous jobs or work situations that are serving you well now?

3

THE MYTH OF BALANCE: LIFE ON THE SEESAW

Brains & Beauty-ism #3
Balance doesn't exist. Get over it.

Arguably, one of the most searched subjects is *work/life balance*. It's also a frequent topic at school drop-offs, cocktail parties, girlfriend lunches, and—I suspect, but can't know for sure—therapy sessions. This is not because we are a world of bratty people who want it all; it's because we have many aspects to our lives, and we want to do them all well without coming apart at the seams.

The subject came up over and over in our *Where Brains Meet Beauty* podcast conversations. For the entrepreneurs I spoke with, it was often given as the reason they went indie—it certainly was for me—foolishly thinking that running our own businesses would provide more time and flexibility than working for a corporation or helping to build someone else's dream. But here's the thing: There is no work/life balance, and maybe we would all be happier if we stopped chasing it. Instead, we should develop some coping skills and helpful habits for juggling the different parts of our lives without losing our minds—and without feeling as if we are failing at all of it.

The metaphor of the seesaw came up in more than one discussion. A seesaw is never static, never in perfect balance. Sometimes you're up, sometimes you're down, and most of the time, you're moving from one to the other. The best you can do is hope that you're not stuck at the top or at the bottom for too long. And that you make the most of each position you find yourself in.

I was moved by my conversation with each guest, and have tremendous respect for the struggle to juggle that is daily life for so many—corporate, indie, parent, all of the above, or en route to these roles. As you read their stories, remember that behind each is a brave soul simply trying not to fall off the seesaw. ❖

"Most days, I'm not getting an A in every-thing, but that's OK."

—Stephanie Kramer
SVP, global marketing and product innovation, SkinCeuticals
(Episode 140)

Stephanie Kramer was our first podcast guest—but not the last—to use the metaphor of the seesaw in describing the elusive work/life balance. In her words, "It's never perfectly balanced, but each side gets to be up sometimes and down sometimes, and it balances out." She described, in a nutshell, the dilemma of how to grow your career while growing your family and growing yourself that so many of us—especially women—face. The key is to make the time away from work matter—to focus on reading to your kids without checking your phone every minute. There will always be some days you get an A in parenting, and some days you get a C. Accept it.

While Stephanie has spent much of her career in the corporate world, she is hardly your typical corporate executive. She calls herself an intrapreneur, strategically using her position to build an entrepreneurial culture within the corporate behemoth. Recognizing that companies big and small need to support their greatest resource—their people—at every stage of life, she has carved out an environment where she can mentor talent, build cross-department alliances, and create flexible schedules and deadlines for her team. That means, for example, that someone training for the marathon can run in daylight, or a parent can attend a child's school play.

Stephanie is a true champion for creating a corporate world that can be more responsive, more sensitive, and more flexible; it just needs someone like her to make it happen. Even in our increasingly enlightened times, Stephanie's management style is unusual. She is hopeful that others will follow her lead, which illustrates that it really is possible to get the work done, even from home during naptime. ❖

"If you don't ask, you won't get what you're looking for."

—Maura Cannon Dick
CMO, FitSkin
(Episode 115)

Maura Cannon Dick did what so many wish they could: worked for years in super-demanding corporate marketing positions, left to focus on her family, then built a consulting business on her own terms. After over twelve years in marketing positions for various Estée Lauder brands, including Clinique and Origins, she decided she needed a break. She took it after her second child was born when she realized that international trips and conference calls at all hours were just not going to work for her anymore. But knowing that she would return to the beauty business eventually, while she was "on break" she kept her skills sharp and her network current to make the road back less bumpy.

Treasuring the time with her family and for herself, Maura knew *when* she was ready to go back, and she knew *how* she wanted to go back—as a consultant who could call the shots. Aware that you can't always control the pipeline of clients and projects when you're essentially a freelancer, Maura's years at Lauder had given her the expertise and confidence to believe that she could build a consulting business that was flexible enough to keep her in the game, yet have time for her family. Still, she wasn't sure at the beginning how it would all play out. But, as she advised our podcast listeners, you can't get what you're looking for if you don't at least ask. So she asked. Reflecting on the lead-up to her agonizing decision to leave a job she loved and rethink her career, Maura advises others who are contemplating such a shift: "It's important to try to test the waters and see what the best fit is for you. There is a great fit for everybody out there. . . . Take the leap and do it."

Now operating advisor for North Castle Partners, CMO of FitSkin, and a consultant at MAC Cosmetics, Maura cites her calendar as one of the keys to her successful balancing act. She views it—and by extension, her life—as a puzzle. By carefully plugging in the puzzle pieces that make her schedule work, she knows when it's work time, when it's kid time, when it's family dinnertime, when it's Maura time. Approaching her calendar with military precision lets her focus on the moment without worrying about the next one. Knowing that even the best laid military plan might need some adjusting for an earache, a flat tire, or a no-show babysitter, her calendar is the key to making her busy life hum. Rather than limiting her, she sees this kind of structure as liberating. Maura would not describe her life as perfect, and it doesn't have a lot of room for spontaneity. But it works more than it doesn't work—and that's a lot. ❖

"Mostly everything can wait until the next business day."

—Dana Jackson
Founder & CEO, Beneath Your Mask
(Episode 186)

Skincare and hair care brand developer Dana Jackson learned the lessons of the seesaw the hard way—the very hard way. Stuck in a high-pressure, twenty-four-seven job, managing finances for big-time celebrities, she experienced a slow-motion crash-and-burn that led to a life-threatening illness. As she began the long, slow road to recovery, she started researching products and ingredients that could heal the skin and hair issues that came along with the lupus nephritis that almost killed her. Not finding what she needed, and definitely not going back to that toxic job, she listened to the voice of the latent entrepreneur lurking inside her and decided to make the products herself. Dana's story is one we often hear: a business launched to solve a personal problem that the marketplace couldn't.

What Dana discovered—what so many entrepreneurs discover in those early, starting-from-zero years—is that there is still plenty of stress in trying to launch a business. It's a different kind of stress, coming from you and your goals rather than from a boss or a corporation, but it's still stress. Having come so close to the edge, she approached this pressure with some perspective on managing the endless demands of developing products and launching a business, summed up in the quote above. She spoke about learning how to prioritize, even in the infancy of your business, when it feels as if every single thing is of make-or-break importance.

Dana shared an anecdote about Beneath Your Mask's wildly popular lip balm that had been out of stock. When they finally received the shipment, the old Dana would have gone without sleep for a week and pressured her whole team to do the same to frantically ship them at warp speed. But instead, everyone calmed down and worked at a brisk but reasonable pace to get the product out the door to customers. Dana poignantly sums up the lesson learned: "Selling a million lip balms is not worth my kidney." ❖

*"There are worse things in life
than the shampoo shipping late."*

—John Costanza
CEO, Beauty Quest Group
(Episode 134)

John Costanza knows the hair care industry inside and out, from his early brand-building days at Joico, to his current position as CEO of Beauty Quest Group, a spinoff from Conair, where he was VP and GM of the Global Salon Professional Division. His impressive resume also includes Sally Beauty and L'Oreal.

But beyond his glowing credentials, John is a unique industry leader who struggled with achieving a work/life balance before most management supported it. As he was climbing the ladder, John found himself in the world of planes, trains, and automobiles a lot more than he wanted to be. He hated leaving his wife and three young children all the time, but as he helped grow Joico, that's what his life became. He couldn't even vent his unhappiness with colleagues since top executives were not supposed to worry about stuff like that. You were working to support your family, and time away from them was simply the cost. The message was: deal with it. And if you were a man, the quest for balance was frowned upon even more. In the early years of his career, the double standard was fully operational.

After a long travel-intensive stint with Sally Beauty, L'Oreal came calling with an offer as GM for two of its brands, based in New York. The Big Decision was upon him. He knew what a huge opportunity it was. His kids were older, though still at home, and he knew it was time to take the leap if he wanted to move to the next level professionally. So the family relocated to a house in New Jersey while John commuted to his office in Manhattan every day. It did not take long for his family—initially so excited about the move—to realize that New Jersey is not New York City. The adjustments were major.

Perhaps the speed bumps that arose during this move helped John focus on what's really important in his work and his life. Lesson #1: Lost time with family you never get back. Lesson #2: Don't stress too much about whether the shampoo will ship on time. Lesson #3: Balance and perspective are essential to being an effective and supportive leader. And the overarching message for John: no regrets. There's a reason for every experience. As he put it, "You soak it in, learn from it, then move on, and it usually makes you a stronger person." Lessons well learned, indeed. ❖

"I think every day, we're trying to balance."

—Sasha Plavsic
Founder, ILIA Beauty
(Episode 145)

Niche skincare line ILIA Beauty is a hybrid of organic ingredients and carefully curated, safe synthetics that can often boost efficacy. Founder Sasha Plavsic traces the origins of her concept for ILIA to her "Saturn Return" moment—the time when Saturn returns to the position it was in when you were born, around your late twenties, often a time of major growth or change. Sasha describes it as a time "when we start to grow up and realize that we don't have to please everybody." It was definitely eye-opening for the twenty-eight-year-old Sasha, who became curious about lots of things, including the ingredients in the beauty products she used. ILIA evolved from there.

At the time of her podcast recording, Sasha had just completed a rebranding of the skin-centric makeup line. It had been nine years since launch, and it was clearly time for an update. But it also involved letting go of a lot of her past, and she felt as if she was losing an old friend. Entrepreneurs and parents can probably relate.

Of course, you want your business to grow from that initial idea, started at your kitchen table, to a humming-along operation with a team of professionals to help you realize your dream. Of course, you want your baby to grow and thrive, but with each stage, you miss the one that came before, from the baby to the toddler to the preschooler, and then the kindergartener who tugs at your heart as you wave goodbye at the classroom door. Huge adjustments all around. That's how Sasha felt as she was saying goodbye to the original packaging and messaging that she had created from nothing. She was thrilled with the results, but she felt as if she had been in a kind of mourning. She finally realized that it's okay and natural to feel sadness and fear as things change.

Sasha was the second podcast guest in as many weeks who spoke of the metaphor of the seesaw and its delicate balance. She sees the struggle to attain balance as the antidote to the struggle to achieve the (unachievable) goal of trying to be everything to everyone at every moment—a particular illusion for women. She concludes, "You shouldn't be hard on yourself if you feel like you're going to knock out of balance, because you will. We have to know that if we can strive toward [balance], that's what matters." Sasha feels it's vital to see that life, like the playground classic, is never perfectly balanced. You learn to manage the ups and downs. And once in a while, it's okay—in fact, it's essential—to slow down, turn off the phone, and enjoy the ride. ❖

"You must ruthlessly prioritize."

—Laura Schubert
CEO and co-founder, Fur
(Episode 136)

After years in the corporate world, Laura Schubert had had it. While she admits that the lessons she learned in leadership as a strategic management consultant for major corporations, including Goldman Sachs and Bain Consulting, are serving her well as an entrepreneur, she also admits that she was miserable. She had been working on a disruptive business concept—grooming products for one's most intimate places—that was about as niche an idea as you can get (literally), and wanted to take the plunge. No matter that she launched the business as she was about to have a baby. When the muse visited her, she was ready.

Laura has a fascinating mantra: ruthless prioritization. Many working moms, especially new working moms, get overwhelmed by all there is to juggle. Laura uses this mantra to constantly question if she is really, truly, absolutely working on the most important thing she could be working on at that moment— sometimes checking herself every hour to help her stay focused. In her words, "When I get to work, I have these eight hours to do the most important things that need to get done that day. That's all I do, and then I'm gone."

She believes the habit of ruthless prioritization has made her a better leader and a better manager—and probably a better mom, too, since when she is with her child, she is 100 percent present.

She observes that working moms prioritize all the time because they must, although they might not all do it as ruthlessly as Laura does. But they know how to focus, how to use the limited time they have to complete tasks, and how to help team members do the same. The takeaway from Laura's story could be: Looking for leadership? Looking for productivity? Hire a mom. ❖

MY SEESAW

My seesaw moment came after I gave birth to my second child. Base Beauty's biggest client was a global prestige beauty brand, a wonderful relationship with a high-profile client and lovely people. I was pregnant when we started working with them, so they generally knew when I was due. The day after my daughter was born, while I was still in the hospital, I got an email from my client contact to ask if we would work on a big project. (I'm using the term "we" loosely here since our agency was still small; the "we" was pretty much me since I had no one to hand this off to.) I said I'd love to work on it, not really worried about how to get it done with a new-born since this was my second child, and I wasn't over-whelmed by the new baby routine. But when I said yes to the assignment, I did not mention my daughter's birth, fearing they would judge me for taking the work with a brand-new baby in my arms. What I didn't learn until later was that the client team had been worried about me. They knew I was near the end of my pregnancy, and when they didn't hear the news of my daughter's birth, they thought something might have happened. Here I was hiding the news, afraid they would judge me for not taking maternity leave, or would assume I couldn't handle their project. Even with all I had on my plate, my seesaw was pretty well balanced, and I knew I could handle the work. But the larger point is that I didn't have the confidence to stand proudly behind my decision at that moment. What I realized is that I had clients who cared about me and my family's well-being, who loved working with me, and who were not judging me. Had I shared my news right away, that conversation would have reduced my stress level and my client's concern. ❖

Lesson Learned

Balance is tricky and never perfect, but you'll never come close if you don't talk about it and share the struggle to achieve it with those around you—family, colleagues, even clients. Don't assume people know what you need or won't be responsive to it. They just might surprise you. ❖

SOUND BITES

It's never perfectly balanced, so don't sweat it.

Go home. Do it tomorrow.

Structure can give you freedom.

Moms make great leaders.

You never get time back.

FOOD FOR THOUGHT

➤ How does the work/life balance (or lack thereof) play out in your life?

➤ Have you ever been in a situation where simply speaking up about your circumstances would have relieved the stress? Why did you hesitate? Do you think the people on the other end of that conversation would have understood?

➤ Can you make a list of two or three small things you can easily do to make your life a little more balanced?

THE PURSUIT
OF WELLNESS

Brains & Beauty-ism #4
Entrepreneur, heal thyself.

T here's a theory—maybe it's just my theory—that you could write a pretty complete history of progress if you looked at those unique minds who saw a problem and thought, "Hmm, how can I solve this?" Certainly, this approach would chronicle the beauty and wellness industries. There are countless stories of those who, when not served by conventional medicine or existing products, sought alternatives, reaching for folk remedies, teachings from Eastern medicine, nutritional programs, exercise regimens, or plant and herbal solutions from an array of cultures and traditions. Some worked, some didn't.

And when they didn't, these bold souls, faced with an illness—physical or mental, their own or a loved one's—confronted that illness head-on and went about finding or creating something that would. What makes these stories all the more remarkable is that these entrepreneurs began their quests for answers while still battling the condition, some of which were life-threatening. And for some, this was their first foray into entrepreneurship, essentially building the airplane while flying it. Without question, there is something unique in the DNA of entrepreneurs.

Here are poignant stories of innovation, creativity, and courage from *Where Brains Meet Beauty* podcast guests who have done nothing less than saved themselves and their loved ones, inspiring many of us along the way. ❖

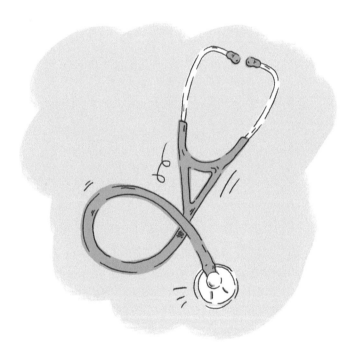

*"I looked at my illness as this opportunity
to create the life I wanted moving forward."*

—Indie Lee
Founder and CEO, Indie Lee & Co.
(Episode 181)

Indie Lee's story could be titled How a Type A Accountant Became a Clean Beauty Expert. It started with a foundation-rocking, life-changing, super scary medical diagnosis: a benign yet still-threatening brain tumor caused by an autoimmune disease. Upon hearing the news, she did a double take. "What?" she thought. "I eat organic. I grow my food in my backyard. How is this possible?" When her neuroendocrinologist suggested her tumor might be tied to the environment, a light bulb clicked in her head. She had only been thinking about what she put into her body, not what she put onto her body. And he told her that he and his colleagues had been seeing an increasing number of such cases.

She saw this diagnosis and its potential causes as a challenge and a calling, and she set out to research and develop a line of *truly* clean skincare products, with ingredients and their sources shared with consumers and presented honestly without hype or greenwashing. She sold her jewelry, maxed her credit cards, emptied her 401(k), and she was off. It's difficult enough to research and launch a skincare business, but imagine doing it while battling a brain tumor, knowing you have a ticking time bomb in your head. Right in the middle of her product development, she took a pit stop for the brain surgery that could have ended her life, but actually saved it. When she woke up from surgery and contemplated the road ahead, she decided to dedicate it to educating and empowering others on science, nature, and what's good—and not so good—for skin. Thus, Indie Lee clean skincare was born.

How Indie studied and experimented and worked with growers and labs to develop her products is impressive. Her journey is a shining example of a personal challenge serving as a springboard for a business, and a poignant story of guts and grit, of survival and triumph. ✤

"Let's age the way we want to
on our own terms. "

—Rochelle Weitzner
CEO and founder, Pause Well-Aging
(Episode 112)

Life in the C-suite was humming along for Rochelle Weitzner. As the former CEO of Erno Laszlo, and former CFO at Laura Mercier Cosmetics and RéVive Skincare, she had spent years improving the bottom lines of brands dedicated to the idea of anti-aging. Then one day, out of the blue, she started sweating for no apparent reason, heat radiating off her reddening face, and she realized she was experiencing her first hot flash. She was a beauty and wellness industry insider, but no one had prepared her for this. She felt alone and confused. She naturally looked to her industry for products that could support her through menopause. What she found—actually, what she didn't find—shocked her. "Not only were there no products targeting the particular effects of menopause on skin," she reflected, "but no one was even talking about it. For all the noise we make about products aimed at anti-aging, it was as if the whole topic of menopause was forbidden."

As a woman experiencing menopause without much cultural support, as well as a savvy beauty executive, Rochelle saw an opportunity to reach an enormous market that had been essentially ignored. She decided to redirect her deep experience in beauty to fill this gaping void. To underscore the lack of menopause awareness, she hysterically recalls the blank stares she received from men when she was raising capital, especially from one older gentleman who, after her twenty-minute, science-heavy pitch, said to her, "I have no idea what you're talking about. I'm going to go home and talk to my wife about it."

Pause Well-Aging is a first-of-its-kind, science-based skincare line focused on supporting skin during the three stages of menopause. But it's also about community, about giving women resources and space to share their stories as they adapt to the "new normal" of menopause that will be a fact for the rest of their lives. Her instincts were spot on. Launched only a few years ago, Pause found its footing right away, discovered by women who were hungry for products and messages that would address their experience.

Not only does Pause offer products that are laser-focused on the particular needs of skin during menopause, but it does so with honesty, compassion, and humor—an approach that is at the core of the culture Rochelle is building around the company. She looks at it this way: Menopause affects, or will affect, half of the people in the world, and women are living longer and better than ever, with active, rich lives, careers, and relationships. Menopause today is not our grandmother's "change of life," whispered in guarded tones—if it was mentioned at all. Rochelle is using her expertise and her products as a platform to open up the conversation and bring menopause out of the shadows. ❖

"Imagine if you made decisions based on what made you happy rather than what you thought made you perfect."

—Poppy Jamie
Founder, Happy Not Perfect
(Episode 79)

By her early twenties, Poppy Jamie was already leading a perfect life. At least, that's what it looked like from the outside. She was a successful TV personality, had her own Snapchat show, and had designed a line of accessories with her best friend, Suki Waterhouse. But underneath the gloss of social media was a different reality—an overworked, always-on existence. The kind that paves the road to burnout. She thought, "Hold on a minute, I don't want to feel this stressed out. I don't want my kids to feel this stressed out." And then, "How do we learn to think better?" She discovered that there's an actual medical diagnosis for what she was experiencing: adrenal fatigue. And she learned from her followers how prevalent it was, especially among women, who often suffer from the "disease to please," or the "good-girl syndrome," spending all our energy trying to please everyone around us without having much left for ourselves.

That diagnosis was her wake-up call. She realized she had to re-evaluate her life and reset her priorities. Early on, she grasped that "perfect is such a confusing word because often it has been created by other people's expectations." Happy Not Perfect is the result of her quest to change her life, and while she was at it, the lives of others. The influence app curates positive, upbeat messages, quotes, reminders, and tips of the day, while helping people filter out the negativity that often gets more attention than the good stuff. To educate herself while building it, she consulted with neuroscientists, CBD specialists, sleep experts, even a breathing coach, funneling all their knowledge into the app, followed by a book.

The deep learning for Poppy is about neuroplasticity, the ability to retrain your brain and change stress-inducing negative ways of reacting. Through simple practices, such as writing down one thing you're grateful for every day or breathing from your belly, not your chest, you can learn to manage the stress, even if you can't eliminate it. Poppy thinks of the app, with its upbeat messaging and exercises, as a kind of gym for the mind. We train for a marathon or a professional goal, so here's a tool to train for happiness.

Poppy acknowledges how social media causes much of today's stress, as we're constantly bombarded with (carefully edited) images of other people's lives, often convincing ourselves that our own is somehow deficient in comparison. She suggests that we become more thoughtful about who we're following and why. Her life has become immeasurably better by doing so. And she strives for perfection no more. ❖

"I knew that the only way to make a difference was to share my story."

—Victoria Watts
Founder, Victorialand Beauty
(Episode 133)

None of the skincare products Victoria Watts tried were addressing her hyperpigmentation and stress-related skin conditions. So she did what entrepreneurs do: she made her own. Months of mixing and blending essential oils and botanical extracts in her kitchen turned into Victorialand Beauty, a line of good-for-you skincare products that have proven to be so effective she can now go without makeup.

But just as the company was off and running, Victoria was presented with another challenge, one far more critical than the condition of her skin. Her son Cyrus was born with a rare disease that has resulted in significant, and at the moment, irreversible, visual impairment. Out of this heartbreak, Victoria found a new calling. Contemplating how the adult Cyrus would navigate the world without sight, her thoughts turned to packaging, something she knew a lot about. Her eureka moment came in watching her toddler "see" by touching. She conceived of putting some type of tactile recognition on her packaging so that someone who is visually impaired or blind could pick up a product from a store shelf and identify it, gaining a huge measure of independence.

Cut to today and the creation of C-Y-R-U-S, the Raised Universal Symbols System that Victoria has developed for use on any consumer product—a system that's more manageable and spatially viable for packaging than Braille. Beyond using C-Y-R-U-S on Victorialand's packaging, Victoria has been working with other brands to help them apply the system to their own products, to make the world more accessible for the over three hundred million people with some kind of visual impairment.

She looks back on the journey so far and remembers how uncertain she was at the beginning. "There's always a new challenge, and I still feel like I fly by the seat of my pants, but it's fulfilling. . . . It's all about learning and stepping out of your comfort zone and doing things that you never thought you would do, but once you do it, you're like, 'Oh, I can totally do this.'" She sums up her mission: "Knowing we can make a positive change for so many people . . . I can't even describe how that feels." ❖

"You have to keep evolving."
—Dr. Patricia Wexler
Ccosmetic dermatologist
(Episode 111)

Having grown up caring for two ill parents, Dr. Patricia Wexler feels she was always headed for a medical career. She can't remember when she didn't want to be a doctor, labeling herself pre-med almost from birth. In addition to caring for her parents, she had to deal with cystic acne as a teen, a heartbreaking condition during those crucial formative years. Not sure which path her studies would take, she knew she was destined to be a helper and a healer. Attending noted Bronx High School of Science in New York sent her on her way early.

Patricia sees her cosmetic dermatology as about much more than vanity. The procedures she offers address self-esteem, whether in teens suffering from acne as she had, or in older patients who want to remain relevant as they age and not be seen or treated as "old." Ageism is real; she's seen it, and she's felt it.

Involved with New York's City Meals on Wheels for thirty-one years, she considers her work aligned with the mission of the program that not only delivers nourishing meals to the homebound, but offers a human connection where many have little social contact. It's almost a kind of therapy. Looking in the mirror is often depressing for the elderly, and depression affects longevity. Her procedures can help.

Practicing for almost thirty years, Patricia has no intention of retiring, and in fact, keeps on growing. She does so by attending specialized conferences, learning about new solutions and equipment, always maintaining her reputation as a pioneer—early in her career, she was among the first to embrace Botox and liposuction—and continuing to explore, and even develop, some of these techniques herself. Her work has taken some interesting twists and turns as she helped create skincare, fragrance, and makeup lines for some of the biggest names in fashion and beauty—Donna Karan, Calvin Klein, Revlon, Almay—and eventually her eponymous line for Bath & Body Works. Somehow always managing to make time for her family, this caring dermatologist passionately offers her patients solutions for issues that she knows firsthand are more than skin-deep. ❖

MY WELLNESS

By the time my second child was a toddler, one would have thought I might have some of the work/life balance stuff figured out. But even though I have always considered myself enlightened, forgiving, and empathetic where others were concerned, I was still being very hard on myself. Base Beauty was about five years old and growing nicely, but I was still micromanaging everything. And now I had two kids—a two-year-old and a five-year-old. I thought I had to be the primary caregiver to everything—the business, my two kids, my family, all without help. And I had to be perfect at everything. The problem was that the reality of "everything" had grown exponentially, both on the home front and at work. I remember taking my toddler to a mommy & me gymnastics program, holding her hand in one of mine as she sat on the mat, and holding my phone in my other hand, emailing clients. I was not engaged or having fun, and was frustrated that this weekday gymnastics class, which was a symbol for the "freedom" I thought I would achieve as an entrepreneur, was actually a super stressful weekly event. My heart was racing all the time, and I was probably on track to make myself really sick. It took me a long time to give myself permission to put the phone away for an hour and get a sitter for a few hours a week to help out. It had nothing to do with money. I thought it would be a sign of weakness, or that I would be missing out on important moments. But if I wasn't fully present when I was with my kids, wasn't I already missing out? ✤

Lesson Learned

Asking for help is not a sign of weakness. It is actually a sign of strength and resilience, and a way to care for those you love, yourself included. ✤

SOUND BITES

You can retrain your brain.

Perfection is a word created by other people's expectations.

Always dig deeper.

Pursuing perfection is like walking through life with a really heavy backpack.

Doing your best might just be enough.

Control what you can, which is not that much.

FOOD FOR THOUGHT

➤ Did you ever experience a period of stress that turned out to be a wake-up call to make some changes to protect or improve your health?

➤ How much "me" time do you have? Can you find a way to build in some consistent time for self-care, even if it's only a few minutes a day?

➤ Have you ever forced yourself to put down your phone or turn off your computer to enjoy an experience fully? If not, have you ever thought about doing it?

5

TRUTH *AND* CONSEQUENCES

Brains & Beauty-ism #5
Go with your gut—and your heart.

There are thousands of pithy quotes from writers, scholars, philosophers, and statesmen on being true to oneself and one's beliefs. I know these words resonate with our *Where Brains Meet Beauty* podcast guests. Perhaps that's because they form a community of individuals—call them mavericks or renegades or visionaries—who listened to their inner voice, whispering or screaming, telling them that there was something more out there. They're the scrappy ones who left a job, left a home, maxed their credit cards, and set up shop, taking a risk to pursue a dream. Many guests told me that one motivator for starting their own business was the opportunity to build in their values and create a culture that reflected what was important to them beyond the products or services they were selling. They wanted meaning in their work. Becoming your own boss is the ultimate do-over.

As an entrepreneur, I instantly relate to the stories of other entrepreneurs. Still, I've also worked for large companies and am equally fascinated by how enlightened corporate executives can implement their values in an environment that's much harder to control and change. Often there are thick manuals outlining structures, rules, and policies that dictate how every employee should behave. Those who stand up to all of that are brave indeed.

Many outside the beauty arena may view our work as fluffy and superficial (comments often made while running out to get the newest moisturizer or mascara!). But in talking to these beauty leaders, I saw how thoughtful and value-driven they are. In conceiving their indie companies or running their corporate departments, they continually strive to live truly authentic lives. And they have also learned that, more and more, customers are shopping according to their values and can sense hypocrisy a mile away. Brands and marketers must make sure their values are reflected genuinely in every customer touchpoint. As you read these stories, you'll see that these folks are doing exactly that, and that fluff is nowhere to be found. ❖

> *"I was [between] a rock and a hard place. I couldn't take pills and I couldn't not take pills. So I knew that something had to give."*
>
> —Dr. Gregory Brown
> Founder, RéVive Skincare
> (Episode 122)

Most people would have thought that a Harvard medical degree, a thriving plastic surgery practice, and morphing the latest biotech discoveries into a successful skincare start-up would add up to a charmed life. For Dr. Gregory Brown, that outer success masked inner turmoil as he weathered storms—both professional and personal—that would flatten many of us.

After medical school, when he was ready to hang out his shingle for his plastic surgery practice, Gregory did so in his hometown of Louisville, Kentucky, wanting to be close to his family and his roots. But that locale presented some challenges for a gay man living and practicing medicine in an ultra-conservative Southern community in the early days of the AIDS epidemic. He knew how he would be treated, so he kept up appearances at deep personal cost. He describes the feelings: "When you're not living an authentic life for who you are, there's all kinds of pressure because you're not being honest with the world or yourself. Dishonesty is a hard way to live."

As he was growing his practice, he connected with a group of scientists who were just starting to develop human growth factors for use in treating burns and healing wounds. The story of how he evolved that biotech research into RéVive Skincare is an impressive one. Eventually, he gave up his practice to focus on RéVive full time.

RéVive was flourishing, but Gregory wasn't. The accumulated pressures of entrepreneurship and living a closeted existence, along with developing rheumatoid arthritis, eventually led to the major speed bump of addiction. In retrospect, he views his addiction to the non-opiate painkillers he was taking as one of the best things that ever happened to him, helping him "come clean" on more than one front. "It was very difficult to go through at the time. But having come through it and been in recovery all these years has made me a much different person than I think I would've been." Now over fifteen years sober, Gregory shared his story in raw and honest ways, revealing how his journey to sobriety led him to come out and finally start living an authentic life. ❖

"You have to be respectful in how you speak up, but you have to speak your truth."
—Danya Klein
Vice president of brand relations, Preen.Me
(Episode 82)

Having worked for the big guys in beauty at Estée Lauder on the La Mer, Jo Malone, and Clinique brands, and now at indie social research, strategy, and activation firm Preen.Me, Danya Klein knows the beauty world from all sides. She shared three stories that were pivotal in her entry into beauty and her success once there.

Story #1: A friend pushed her to study Mandarin in college, observing that China was rising as a major global market. So she did, for three years, then boldly moved to China for two years to test and complete her basic classroom grasp of the language. Just struggling to get by in a very foreign land in the nineties was challenging enough for this girl from suburban New Jersey. But while there, she had to have an emergency appendectomy, which, among other things, shifted her language skills into high gear. It was no longer a question of adding a language to her resume. She describes, "It went from being a pursuit of trying to win over my ego and speak intelligently in Chinese, to just having to survive in the hospital, and that's how I started to speak." When she returned to the States, she was fluent.

Story #2: Upon her return, looking for a job, any job, she had an entrée to the head of Estée Lauder International, who was very impressed at the bold step Danya had taken by moving to China when she did. Not only that, it turned out that Danya had worked in a hotel in which this woman's husband had had a heart attack while in China on business, and for whatever reason, that coincidence sealed the deal; she was hired to work on the Clinique brand's expansion into China.

Story #3: Danya was given great exposure at Clinique. She is grateful to some wonderful mentors who valued her experience in China and listened to what their twenty-two-year-old newbie had to say. One day, she was in a photo review for the launch of the brand's Stop Signs anti-aging line in the Asia-Pacific market, shot by the legendary Irving Penn. Danya had not been at the shoot, but the first time she saw the test shots, she gasped. One was a picture of a cupcake with four white blown-out candles. Everyone at the meeting was oohing and aahing, and she had to steel herself to speak up. She needed to explain that the number four symbolized death in Chinese culture, and that white is the color for funerals, so their campaign with the four used candles was giving women a message of death. It was hard, but she got the words out, addressing the meeting: "I don't think that's what you want to tell a woman the first time she's experiencing Clinique anti-aging skincare." They reshot the campaign with color, and while it was not expressly acknowledged, the leadership knew that their young team member had saved them from a costly and embarrassing mistake.

No one has to school Danya on the importance of speaking up and speaking truth, in any language. ❖

*"I don't want to make stuff just for
the sake of making stuff."*

—Leslie Harris
Global general manager, SkinCeuticals
(Episode 183)

Leslie Harris has always been extremely picky about where she works. Perhaps that explains why her path to the beauty world—and to a particular space within the beauty world—has been a zigzagging one. Starting in finance, then swerving to academia, then pivoting to beauty, Leslie has been thoughtful at every turn. One of those turns was a detour across the pond to study at the London College of Fashion, focusing on the intersection of fashion, culture, and beauty. While there, she was drawn to exploring really specific, quirky topics—such as, how fashion was used to sell cars to women between the world wars—and discovered that she has a talent for taking things that are seemingly unrelated and finding ways to connect them. That's where Leslie finds the fun.

The thread that weaves her career choices together is her search to find meaning in her work, whatever that work might be. That meant that when she was considering the beauty industry, she had to find a role that was about more than pushing the newest shade of lipstick or peddling a lot of stuff that people didn't really need. Skincare was where she landed since it's about solving problems. And SkinCeuticals, with its mission to improve skin health with honest, science-backed products, was a perfect fit. She observes, "I'm not a person who could work for just any brand. . . . You have to think about the good you put back in the world."

Leslie is the first to speak up when people talk about the beauty industry as superficial or vacuous. She points out that there are many companies, hers included, making fine products that solve problems, improve lives, and help customers feel better about themselves. And for her, nothing could be more meaningful than that. ❖

---

*"I have a holistic approach to sustainability. . . .
How do we mitigate harm? How do we
do fewer bad things?"*

—Dr. Zahir Dossa
CEO and co-founder, Function of Beauty
(Episode 177)

The beauty industry was nowhere on the radar screen for the young Zahir Dossa. His childhood dream was of becoming an astronaut—hopes dashed early on for some minor-to-him but major-to-NASA physical conditions, including childhood asthma (outgrown) and less-than-perfect vision (no glasses in space). But he was always a big-picture thinker, so he figured he'd just downsize his dream, from saving the universe to saving the earth.

The story of how he pivoted from that far-out goal to leading a personalized beauty products company is a long one, with intriguing twists and turns. But when you step back, it makes sense. After he recovered from his deep disappointment in not going to space, he managed to fulfill another childhood dream that he admits was kind of a weird goal for a kid—going to MIT. He fulfilled this one in triplicate with a bachelor of science in management, a master of engineering in computer science, and a doctor of philosophy in sustainable development from the famed university. As stated, he's always looking at the big picture.

Throughout his studies, especially as he worked on his doctorate, Zahir focused on broadening the thinking around sustainability, "not just for the environment, but for society and the economy," as he puts it. He studied companies having positive impacts on the world beyond simply implementing better recycling programs than the other guys.

The leap from academia to hair care was bridged by a program he was involved in starting as part of his doctoral studies—an argan oil cooperative in Morocco. He became fascinated by how it grew to provide livelihoods for sixty women who produced and sold goods directly to consumers. That was the catalyst for other products, and a business model that took advantage of his engineering background to create a personalized hair care system. All along the way, sustainability has been top-of-mind.

Not surprisingly, woven into the fabric of Function of Beauty is a strong sense of social responsibility, realized through the company's support of Girlstart, an organization that gives girls more access to STEM studies. And to make sure his greater global goals don't get lost in the world of shampoo and moisturizer, Zahir started a foundation as an outlet for his other passions and ideas. Some of its projects? Regrowing coral reefs. Poverty alleviation. Expansive, conceptual thinking, always. It's pretty clear that Zahir has a mind and a mission to make a real impact. He may not be the astronaut he once dreamed of, but he's soaring just the same. ❖

> *"I'm loyal to brands. I don't jump from one to another."*
>
> —Bart Kaczanowicz
> Founder, OMGBart.com
> (Episode 126)

Founder of the high-end skincare blog OMGBart.com, Bart Kaczanowicz thinks of himself as a curator more than just an influencer. He never vouches for a product he has not used over time and does not truly believe in. He's aware of influencers who accept every product offered and write posts based on trends or money rather than their actual results. For Bart, it's not about numbers—it's about authenticity. And his followers can tell. That's why he has become a jewel of an influencer, trusted by brands and fans. It's been suggested that an appropriate nickname for his blog would be TrustBart.com.

Bart's road to his work in skincare was a twisty, turny one. Born in Poland, he first set foot in America at seventeen, as a high school exchange student in Southern California. He talks about the impact of leaving gray Poland for the sunny

California he had seen on TV in the show *Beverly Hills 90210*. Unsurprisingly, major culture shock ensued.

It was a series of hits and misses that helped Bart discover his passion for skincare. Once he did, he bombarded every major company he could think of with resumés, always sending them priority mail, so someone had to actually look at it. With his I'll-do-anything attitude, he got a foot in the door at Lauder and was on his way.

Anyone would be impressed with Bart's thoughtfulness and respect for the products in his care and on his shelves. He takes his responsibility seriously, posting his honest results based on products he has used for a while. "I will make sure that I will always use something that works for me. . . . I'm loyal to formulas and brands, but I will also tell a brand that this new launch is definitely not for me. If I can politely decline, I will happily do so." This honesty is what makes him such a valuable resource, guiding followers to the latest in luxury skincare, vetted according to his high standards and genuine evaluations. In a world flooded with fakes, skincare influencer Bart stands out as the real deal. ❖

"If it doesn't feel right, don't do it."
—Taryn Toomey
Founder and CEO, The Class
(Episode 92)

Note: In January 2019, when *Where Brains Meet Beauty* was celebrating its second anniversary, we launched the first episode as part of our collaboration with Saks Fifth Avenue. The podcast was recorded in front of an audience on the expansive new beauty floor at Saks' flagship store in Manhattan. Taryn Toomey was our guest for that first episode that launched the monthly podcast-in-residence series.

Just like the mindful workout she has created, Taryn Toomey is an original. Because no one, including Taryn, could come up with a name that would adequately describe it, she calls it simply The Class. It has been featured in *Vogue* and *The New York Times,* and has built a global presence through The Class Digital Studio. In The Class, Taryn leads an unexpected and unexplainable workout, guiding clients on a deep, personal journey that helps them connect with their whole selves—physical, emotional, mental, spiritual—to reach a higher purpose and greater fulfillment. Because it is so challenging to describe, it ends up sounding like touchy-feely hype when one tries. But for those who have experienced it, including some of the *Where Brains Meet Beauty* team, it is nothing less than mind-blowing.

The seeds of Taryn's journey to The Class were sown after she left a career in fashion and was going through a period of personal loss and hardship. She developed her approach organically, trying things that felt right and felt good while she was grieving and healing. As she progressed, she realized that she could pull together the things that worked for her to create a way to help others.

Self-taught through studying the connections between the physical and the emotional, Taryn lights up when she talks about The Class—excitement witnessed as she faced a live audience during the Saks recording. She described how a component such as squatting for the total duration of a song can focus the mind and connect the feelings with the body, helping us to retrain our brains as we retrain our muscles. The mat-based, music-driven workout is structured so that one move is repeated through the duration of a song to create the sensation in the body and focus one's thoughts. Her elevator pitch begins, "The Class is a mind-body cathartic workout where we intentionally engage discomfort in the physical body to close the eyes and witness what the mind does around the feeling. And in that space, we will track different thoughts that we've had. We'll notice how long we've had that thought about the feeling, and then understand the power of choice."

According to Taryn, we all need to open up our thoughts and feelings, and she thinks of movement and music as medicine that helps us achieve the overarching goal of self-awareness. Each person essentially guides their own Class from within and has their own experience during it. Taryn is simply the dynamic catalyst who speaks from her heart, genuinely and generously inviting participants to listen to and learn about themselves. ❖

*"I think to be successful . . . you have
to have a good, kind soul."*
—David Pirrotta
Founder and CEO, David Pirrotta Brands
(Episode 148)

Studying musical theater in college, with his eye on Broadway, brand builder extraordinaire David Pirotta now sees that he was destined for the beauty industry. Growing up, he had a fun, fabulous, larger-than-life aunt who took him to all the department store beauty counters, a mom who loved beauty, and a Cuban grandmother who made her own natural beauty products and soaps. Having learned about stage makeup as part of his theater training, he was able to start his beauty career at the Bergdorf Goodman beauty counter, where he met big-time creative directors, models, and celebrities. He was hooked.

David uses his "nose" and his gut to differentiate those fledgling beauty brands that are good enough, from the ones that are game-changing. Once he takes on brands he thinks are headed for stardom, he helps them get there, advising on everything from early financial challenges to getting the UPCs printed on the packaging to planning a start-small retail strategy, making sure the newbies cover all the bases. Like a proud papa, David coaches and nurtures, helping baby brands find their footing on the big stage.

As he sifts through all the start-up brands that come knocking on his door, looking for guidance, David has come up with a trio of criteria that he equates to the triple threat in musical theater. For Broadway, you have to sing, dance, and act. To sign on with David Pirrotta Brands, you also have to have the triple threat: stellar packaging, a differentiating brand story, and integrity in your ingredients. In almost twelve years, his company has helped launch over eighty brands. It's no surprise that he's called "the brand whisperer."

With his gift for sensing what's unique about a brand and exploiting it in a good way, David offers an invaluable service to young brands. The most important part of that service is honesty. "People come to me for honesty. I don't just tell you what you want to hear." But David and his team always mix the sometimes-hard-to-hear truth with kindness, making it easier for those starting out to grasp without being completely deflated. He has saved many brands from expensive, embarrassing, or fatal mistakes. This artful mix of honesty and kindness is just what you need when you're launching your dream. ❖

MY TRUTH

In considering how to be true to one's values in business, one of the most important values for me is empathy. Maybe today's business schools talk about leading with empathy, but it was not something I was taught formally. It is top-of-mind for me in every interaction in business—with my team, with my clients, and with their customers. The poignant metaphor of walking a mile in another's shoes to really understand who they are and what they need is meaningful for me. I think my empathy grew out of those early jobs and temp gigs where I experienced what it felt like not to be heard or truly valued.

So as Base Beauty continues to grow, as we choose which clients are the best fit for us, and as our team expands, empathy is a key barometer. I can sense which clients, brands, and products really care about authentic messaging that focuses on what customers need. I'm good at finding team members who grasp our core values of openness, respect, pride in our work, and support of each other. As they move into leadership roles, they, in turn, build their departments with like-minded new hires, and these values become baked into the agency's DNA. That produces better work for our clients and an agency credo we can be proud of.

Here are some examples of how empathy is woven into Base Beauty's core values:

- In planning how to spend a client's budget, I think of it as money coming out of my own pocket. That ensures their money goes where it's the most impactful.

- If a team member presents work that doesn't meet our standards, we work with them to figure out why, empowering them to be part of the process by making sure the task was understood and assessing any roadblocks they might have met. These are crucial teaching moments that build confidence and develop skills.

- We celebrate side hustles. Many of our team members have passions outside of their work with us that we love to honor. We try to embrace whatever talented people bring to the table. People are more fulfilled, more well-rounded, and more loyal. Plus, their outside interests always reap benefits for BBCA, often in unexpected ways.

- We put ourselves in the customer's shoes. With fewer in-person beauty moments or events these days, brands are challenged to reach their customers. As we plan how to connect with customers digitally, we think about what they need to know to make a purchasing decision. When we are concepting a program for a client, I always ask my team the question we need to answer for customers standing in the store or shopping on their computers or phones: "Why should I care about this product?" By empathizing with them, we can show customers why they should care. ✤

Lesson Learned

We work from a place of empathy. We put ourselves in our client's place, the customer's place, each team member's place. How would each of them want to be valued and treated? This approach results in happy clients, satisfied customers, and a fulfilled BBCA team where everyone feels good about delivering authentic creative work. ✤

SOUND BITES

Everything is an audition.

Everything is a performance.

You can be authentic anywhere.

Look beyond the checked boxes.

Speak up.

Speak your truth.

FOOD FOR THOUGHT

➤ Have you ever put yourself in someone else's shoes to improve the outcome of a difficult interaction? How did it work out?

➤ Are you in a position to build your values into your business, your work, or even your job? What are some of the concrete ways in which you have done that?

➤ Can you remember a situation where it was challenging to speak up and speak the truth, but you did it anyway? What was the result?

6

SCREWING UP, BOUNCING BACK, MOVING ON

Brains & Beauty-ism #6
AFGO (another f***ing growth opportunity)

Corporate heavyweight, disruptive entrepreneur, or some combination of both, everyone encounters setbacks in work and in life. The grace—or lack thereof—with which we face them says a lot about who we are and what will follow. Since the focus of *Where Brains Meet Beauty* is to explore our podcast guests' personal stories as they relate to their professional lives, we hear a lot about those speed bumps. Sometimes they stem from rookie mistakes. Sometimes from circumstances beyond one's control, such as a global pandemic.

Our conversations are just that—I share as much with my guests as they share with me. And there is mutual comfort in hearing about their challenges as I tell them about mine. Even though everyone knows that starting and/or running a business is tough, no one is fully prepared for just how tough. Time after time, I sat in awe as I learned how each guest navigated the often-jagged path before them, whether launching a product line, facing an unraveling industry segment, or encountering prejudice.

The pandemic affected the beauty industry in major ways—shutting down salons; halting orders for the supplies they use; canceling dress-up events; curtailing the need for makeup, as so many were working from home. And for those who did venture back into stores, the testing and sampling that are so crucial to cosmetic sales were limited or eliminated. I was moved by how the beauty industry responded, finding creative ways to stay afloat, even reaching out to competitors to combine resources.

A hysterical acronym on the subject of resilience is AFGO, another f***ing growth opportunity. It speaks to the importance of learning from mistakes and keeping your sense of humor as you do. Read these stories. Grace is everywhere. ❖

> *"COVID has shown us that people want to be a bit more collaborative and open."*
>
> —Priya Rao
> Executive editor, Glossy and host of the Glossy Beauty Podcast
> (Episode 170)

Growing up in a small town in south Texas where hers was one of the very few Indian families, Priya Rao always felt like an outsider, and that she had to prove herself more than her classmates. Headed for a nice, stable (and boring) career in banking, she had a sitcom-worthy roommate situation that opened her eyes to the world of creative pursuits. She realized that if she was willing to journey off the beaten path, she could lead a more exciting career—so she did.

Starting with the fashion merchandising program at Gap, Inc., she has since worked at nearly every beauty and fashion magazine out there. She has constantly been at the intersection of publishing and beauty, a crossroad that leads to parties, media events, networking, and sometimes endless small talk—none of which is her forte. She loves her work but has never fully embraced all the industry pomp and circumstance, still feeling like an outsider, although she definitely is not. But she always knew from the companies she worked for—*Women's Wear Daily, The Wall Street Journal, Town & Country, Harper's Bazaar, Vanity Fair, InStyle*—that there was a hierarchy, a structure, as well as a pedigree and a "look" that one had to fit into. She also knew that "I wasn't going to be the person who was put on *The Today Show,* because I didn't look a certain way . . . The industry wasn't ready for that kind of change at the time."

But change began to happen, albeit slowly. Then the pandemic and the Black Lives Matter movement came along and provided a necessary reset in thinking and openness across the publishing and beauty industries. Priya now appreciates connecting with people on a different level—one that doesn't involve cocktail parties, launch dinners, or free facials as brands pitch her for coverage. While she is grateful for her deep background inside the legacy publishing companies, this "outsider" is even more grateful that she has been able to set her own course. ❖

"There are stories to tell everywhere. "

—Jessica Matlin and Jennifer Goldstein Sullivan
Hosts, Fat Mascara podcast
(Episode 28)

Jessica Matlin and Jennifer (née Goldstein) Sullivan started their podcast, *Fat Mascara,* as a fun side hustle from their day jobs as beauty editors—Jess at *Cosmopolitan,* and Jenn at *Marie Claire.* They never dreamed that it would grow into a consistently top-rated beauty podcast. They simply enjoyed it and felt fortunate that their bosses didn't object; on the contrary, they offered you-go-girl support. Much of our discussion focused on sharing experiences, podcast host to podcast hosts, such as how we choose guests, how much to pre-interview so that guests aren't blindsided but can still respond spontaneously, and how our respective podcasts offer channels for stories that can't be covered as fully elsewhere. When it comes to choosing guests, they always like to talk to someone they've met as editors—a kind of vetting process, always looking for someone who brings something different to the table. Jess explained they choose people where, "we had a connection, we saw that there was something else there besides the fact that they make amazing hair cream."

But no one could ignore the elephant in the room: the shrinking of magazine publishing, and the resilience and adaptability necessitated. There was a period a couple of years ago during which beauty editors were getting let go left and right as the industry consolidated and titles shut down or pivoted to online only. While

Jess and Jenn have not been directly affected by this trend, their timing in launching *Fat Mascara* could not have been better. They love having an of-the-moment way to present expanded beauty news and behind-the-scenes views while print coverage dwindles.

They still miss the days when gorgeous, glossy pages and elaborate shoots were the norm, but have accepted that those kinds of features have become too expensive in a world of diminished circulations. Recognizing that now it's all about clicks, these beauty experts and close friends feel fortunate to continue to cover the beauty news in print while embracing a platform for telling longer, richer beauty stories that people obviously still want to hear. ❖

"I listen to everything. Something random might change the whole path of your life and your career."

—Sue Y. Nabi
CEO, Coty
(Episode 127)

When Sue Nabi was our podcast guest, she had pivoted from corporate life as worldwide president of L'Oreal and Lancôme, to the entrepreneurial world, launching Orveda. This skincare line is based on the Ayurvedic philosophy and science that states that the skin has the power to heal by itself. After getting Orveda off the ground, she returned to the C-suite as CEO of Coty, bringing her innovative thinking to this legacy family of brands.

Sue's path to today was a somewhat circuitous one. Though she had studied biochemical engineering and earned an MBA, she always had her eye on fashion, with a few connections that she thought would get her started after completing her studies. But a chance meeting with legendary couturier Yves Saint Laurent changed everything; he told her that with her background, she should go into beauty. She listened, and often thinks about the significance of that encounter.

Spending twenty years at L'Oreal and growing as the company did, Sue recalls the early years of driving around the south of France in a tiny car, peddling hair care products door to door. Her rise to the C-suite was almost meteoric. Once there, many aspects of her life were handled by others, with a team to book her travel, make her hair appointments, and manage all the details of her life. Asked to describe how she felt the day after she left L'Oreal to start Orveda when all that support was gone, she did so in a word: lost. She didn't stay lost for long.

More than many, Sue has perspective from both the top of the corporate ladder and the tiny beginnings of an indie venture. She remarked on how she always responds when the public reaches out to her—rare for someone in the C-suite. "I listen to everything. And I always think everything is a sign. From time to time, people write to you on LinkedIn. Most of the people on my level don't even have a look. I read everything, and I always think, 'Why did this person propose that to me?' And sometimes it changes the whole path of your life and your career. Sometimes it's a super opening in terms of business." Sue has acquired much wisdom from all of it: the importance of being open to new ideas and opportunities; listening to your customers, no matter what level you're at; not getting crazy over what you can't control; and looking beyond the numbers, to the meaning of what you are creating. Good reminders from someone who knows from whence she speaks. ❖

"Just because something doesn't work doesn't mean you're a failure."

—Fiona Stiles

Celebrity makeup artist, founder & creative director, Reed Clarke
(Episode 159)

Fiona Stiles knows a few things about resilience, having had to pivot and rethink her life on multiple fronts, as so many have had to in the age of COVID-19. As a makeup artist who works on A-list celebrities—Jessica Alba, Jennifer Garner, Nicole Richie, Lily Collins, Jessica Chastain, Elizabeth Banks, and Gabrielle Union, among others—major events, and big commercial and film shoots, her bookings evaporated when the pandemic hit. Pre-COVID, she had become accustomed to a certain amount of unpredictability in her work. Event dates and shoot schedules could shift; one day, she might be booked for the glamorous Met Ball, the next for a private makeup session in a home before an executive's business meeting. As Fiona puts it, "The freedom and unpredictability of our job, which is double-sided, is the most exciting part. . . . You don't know what your next job is. It could be incredibly glamorous or fabulous, or it could just be going to someone's house and doing their makeup. But there's a sense of wonder to the unknown." Accepting that need to adapt on the fly, and having reached a certain level in her profession, Fiona was usually as busy as she wanted to be. Nothing prepared her for the total shutdown of her industry and all the industries that supported it.

Along with having one role disappear due to COVID-19, Fiona was asked to take on another—that of teacher to her daughter—one for which she was woefully unprepared, as she suspects many parents were. She had no idea how hard second-grade math is, and that it is taught completely differently from the way she was taught. She's grateful for the time with her daughter, gaining insights into how she learns, and her strengths and challenges. But it is a whole new set of skills, especially for someone like Fiona, who went to art school where she was surrounded by creative types making weird stuff.

Still using a paper datebook to write down her appointments, Fiona shared how hard it has been to stare at the blank pages and not have much of a schedule other than her daughter's school day. One continuing role that has helped her through this challenging time is Reed Clarke, her ultra-curated, multi-brand beauty website that she attends to before and after the school day. This scrappy, resilient woman weathers life's ups and downs by reminding herself to look at things through more than one lens, whether it's the lens of a parent or the lens of a professional. And she always tries to find the learning in her mistakes and missteps and come out on the other side with something beautiful. ❖

> *"Any successful businessperson will tell you that failure is an inevitable part of that path."*
>
> —Julie Wald
> Founder and chief wellness officer, Namaste New York
> (Episode 125)

In true entrepreneurial fashion, where Julie Wald started is nowhere near where she is now. Trained as a clinical social worker, and working with seriously disenfranchised clients, she described how her work would affect her mentally and physically. She dragged herself home each night, desperate for ways to clear her head and relax her body. As she incorporated yoga, meditation, and other disciplines into her own life, it dawned on her that maybe she could use these approaches to reach some of her most challenging clients. She reflects, "I recognized that so many of my clients didn't have the tools or the verbal skills or the awareness to be able to articulate themselves and use language as a way to process and heal, and that we needed to approach their journey from a multidimensional perspective." Frustrated with conventional clinical psychotherapy for some of these cases, she went renegade and sneaked in a few alternate approaches—with results that amazed even her. She built trust, she got clients to open up, she saw their bodies relax. The seeds of her business were sown.

Julie shared how these realizations blossomed into her concierge wellness business, now with a range of clients, including captains of industry and Wall Street heavyweights. Interestingly enough, the tragic 9/11 attacks were a catalyst in growing her clientele, as New Yorkers from every walk of life were struggling to cope and heal. She explains, "Namaste means 'the light in me sees and honors the light in you.' Many of our clients at the very beginning were in the financial industry, and many of them [after 9/11] were on a healing journey and suddenly were open to practices like yoga and meditation, where prior to the trauma of 9/11, I'm not sure that they would have really sought that out."

As she reflects on the universal struggles of entrepreneurship, Julie highlights one crucial lesson: you're going to make mistakes, and you learn as much from them as from your successes—maybe more. It's what you do with that learning that counts. Julie is the guest who introduced the acronym AFGO (another f***ing growth opportunity), with its built-in irony that any entrepreneur immediately grasps. Working with her clients while keeping her mind and body aligned, Julie artfully navigates the speed bumps, always reminding herself that each one is an AFGO. ❖

MY SCREW-UPS

I have certainly had my share of screw-ups. This story is about my missteps, but it's also about those of my employer. One of my first jobs was as assistant to the editor-in-chief of two major fashion and beauty magazines, a job right out of *The Devil Wears Prada*. I ordered her lunch, made her dinner reservations, filled out the health insurance forms for her children. I had expected that this would be an opportunity to learn the magazine publishing business, but it ended up being a lot of grunt and schlep work. I was not very good at it, and I was not really motivated to become good at it. The job was undefined and thankless. But I did my best. On the positive side, it did help me realize that I was not interested in fashion—at least, not in the way that everyone else there was. And I met some good and kind people who went against type in terms of the cutthroat world of fashion magazines. More good news—or so I thought—was that this was a big publisher with many titles, including several major food and lifestyle magazines. I had always been interested in food and the restaurant business. So after I had been there about six months, I thought I would see if there might be a junior position with one of the food titles. I made an appointment with HR and went upstairs for the meeting. I said that I didn't think my current job was a good fit, but expressed my interest in opportunities with the food titles. I got a "we'll see" sort of brush-off answer. By the time I took the elevator back downstairs to my desk, I had been fired. I have never trusted any HR department since. ❖

Lesson Learned

While I'm putting this experience under the heading of my screw-ups for not performing my job that well, I think this was also a screw-up on the part of this publisher. They missed an opportunity to keep and nurture someone with talent and passion for something in their purview. In terms of bouncing back, it took a while. My ego was bruised, and I was upset by the mean way in which this was handled. I vowed that if I were ever in a leadership position, I would give my employees opportunities to pursue what interested them, whenever possible. ❖

SOUND BITES

Struggle is not failure.

It's not just about the numbers.

Listen.

Pressure can kill.

AFGO.

FOOD FOR THOUGHT

➤ Which one of your screw-ups taught you the most?

➤ Has anyone ever made a random comment that changed your thinking or even the course of your career?

➤ When did you learn that mistakes do not equal failure? Or have you?

7

MORE THAN MAKING LIPSTICK

Brains & Beauty-ism #7
"No one does this alone."
(see below)

Beauty is big. Beauty is profitable. The global beauty industry was valued at over $500 billion in mid-2021. It includes multi-brand, multinational conglomerates, and kitchen-table start-ups. It's highly competitive. Its annals are filled with stories of secret and stolen formulas, boardroom maneuvering, not-so-nice takeovers, plus C-suite talent snatching that makes the NFL free-agent bidding wars look like a playground romp. But that's only one side of the story.

Even before COVID-19, but especially since, I have found a remarkable and profoundly moving level of generosity across all segments of the field. This reaching out manifests itself in three ways: sharing, mentoring, and philanthropy.

While the pandemic has impacted everyone, it has hit the beauty industry especially hard with retail closures, product launch holds, and shuttered salons, spas, and fitness studios. But as you'll see in the stories that follow, we have observed amazing acts of goodness and grace as companies that were—and will again be—fierce competitors have put their individual concerns aside and united to support our industry and our communities by sharing resources, ideas, and strategies.

Mentoring has been prevalent in the beauty industry for a long time, as veterans reach out to newbies to help them learn and grow. Some of our *Where Brains Meet Beauty* guests expressed a desire to nurture talent as a motivating factor for wanting to run their own business or corporate department, often to pay it forward in appreciation of someone who had mentored them. It's not just altruism—it's also really smart to find good people and help them grow to support the entire venture.

Philanthropy runs deep in the beauty and wellness world, where leaders know what it means to feel good about how you look and keep yourself and your family clean and healthy, no matter your living circumstances. Those who have achieved a certain level of success and stability feel the need to share in whatever ways they can. That's why you'll see contributions of products and funds from many beauty companies donated to homeless shelters, schools, and other worthy organizations. I believe generosity is baked into the DNA of the industry.

Read these stories, and you'll see, as one guest says, that there is room for lots of companies—and I'll add, lots of people—to succeed. When each of us does well, the industry thrives, and we can make the world a little better and kinder. We are indeed a community. ✤

"We all thrive on community, now more than ever."

—Natasha Cornstein
CEO, Blushington
(Episode 150)

Natasha Cornstein was our first *Where Brains Meet Beauty* guest when we resumed after the COVID-19 shutdown, recording remotely, and navigating some technical glitches in the process. Looking back, she was probably the perfect guest for this slot, since we were all still reeling from a world that had been completely up-ended, in which most business leaders were in crisis management mode. The adrenalin was still pumping, the panic was still washing over us, and we were trying to clear our heads and plan for an unplannable future. Natasha showed us how that could be done.

On Friday, March 13, 2020, she shut down all of Blushington's makeup and beauty lounges in New York, Los Angeles, and Dallas. Since they offer one-on-one, in-your-face, oh-so-personal makeup applications, obviously social distancing was not possible. Plus, the parties, galas, openings, and other events her customers were getting made up to attend were not happening. When she woke up the following Monday morning, she sat at her desk, turned on her computer, and said to herself, "Everything I do today and for the coming days will define whether or not my business survives." No pressure!

Post-COVID-19 survival was not guaranteed for any business since there have been so many unknowns—changing guidelines, multiple waves, conflicting mandates—like one massive moving target. But the ones who had a better shot at surviving and thriving were the ones with creative, adaptable leadership. Natasha is at once strategic and straightforward, and has always believed that communication is essential. So on that fateful Monday morning, she got on the phone with her landlords, her vendors, her insurance company, her accountants, and her team. She laid it out, asking for their support while explaining that if her business survived, it would be good for all of them. Approaching this process thoughtfully, bravely, and optimistically, she treated her business community as partners. She was awed by the response: by the end of the week, she had cut the company's expenses by 81 percent.

Never having been through anything like this (who had?), Natasha took another bold step. Realizing that so many of her beauty industry peers—nail spas, fitness studios, hair salons, the fifty-plus young, female-led brands Blushington sold in its salons—were going through the same thing, she put together a beauty and wellness forum. It made sense to her to create a place for these business leaders to share ideas, resources, experiences, and strategies as they zigged and zagged and tried to keep their heads above water. This group even included some direct competitors— Natasha believing that, in any industry, there's room for more than one success story. It's pretty remarkable how this savvy, resilient leader harnessed the larger beauty community to help everyone get through those dark days. Natasha poignantly and simply summarized the theme of this chapter and of the whole entrepreneur experience, before COVID, during COVID, and hopefully, when COVID is in the rearview mirror: "No one does this alone." ❖

*"At the end of the day, there's
room for all of us."*

—Emily Perez
Director of Safety, Regulatory Claims, Micro Acquisition,
and Integration, L'Oreal
(Episode 192)

Owner of a (virtual) rack full of hats, Emily Perez wears each one proudly. Her work at L'Oreal is multidimensional, as she leads a team of lawyers and scientists in verifying product safety, product claims, and US and international regulatory compliance for businesses the beauty giant is considering acquiring. This challenging position covers a great deal of ground and requires intelligence and diplomacy, among other qualities.

But while she loves her "day job," Emily is truly passionate about her work leading the Women of Color think tank, one of many such programs at L'Oreal that are part of the company's diversity and inclusion efforts. A champion for Latinas in beauty, Emily described how the group emphasizes education, networking, mentorships, and other aspects of corporate life to level the playing field for L'Oreal's Latina employees. In discussing all she hopes to do with this program, she references her own experience as a ten-year-old coming to the US from Brazil, speaking only Portuguese, struggling to learn English and fit in. (She shared her language challenges and how she was placed in an ESL class for Spanish-speaking kids and came home speaking Spanish to her shocked Portuguese-speaking family!) The knowledge that many Latinas have experienced this feeling of being outsiders, wherever they were born, powers Emily's efforts. She uses the think tank to create a sense of belonging and to make L'Oreal a place where everyone is included, and everyone can soar. This is what Emily finds most fulfilling.

And because her very important work at L'Oreal left her a few unfilled hours, other than parenting her two young children, Emily started the Latinas and Beauty Mentorship Group to support Latinas in the beauty and wellness industry. She saw a white space where Latinas—and other women of color— didn't quite know how they fit into corporate America. The program celebrates and elevates the Latina community. Emily may be the ultimate mentor, a woman who knows where she came from and can empathize with others of similar backgrounds. She poignantly describes her mission, both within L'Oreal and beyond: "I've been fortunate enough to create a network that has benefited me really well within the beauty industry. I just want to share. I want to see others succeed." Driven by her personal history and her passion, Emily is doing just that. ❖

"To grow as a leader, you have to trust others before they trust you."

—Jessica Hanson
President and general manager, AmorePacific US
(Episode 42)

Jessica Hanson is the type of boss anyone would want to work for. She's led businesses large and small, but wherever she goes, mentoring her team and teaching them to become leaders is as important to her as spreadsheets and marketing strategies. And she doesn't just talk about it; she actively works at it by scheduling team leadership sessions, offering books and articles that will inform and inspire, encouraging personal and professional development in every way she can. Communication is an essential part of her approach; she tries to keep her door open as much as a C-level executive can.

Trust is a crucial part of mentoring in Jessica's leadership style. She explains, "I talk a lot about trust with my team to help them establish relationships with each other and grow as leaders." She's learned a lot about trust, much of it in her personal life. A rocky, heartbreaking, ultimately successful journey to parenthood through adoption taught her profound lessons in trust. One is the thought above that sometimes you have to take a leap of faith when it comes to trust. In fact, Jessica views that leap of faith as the very essence of trust, and she sees it as a two-way street between those who work for her and their boss.

One really interesting and unusual aspect of Jessica as a mentor is that she applies the same generosity she gives her team to herself. This means eschewing old thoughts of having to be the perfect, all-knowing boss at all times. She definitely has high standards for her work, but not insanely high ones. Gone are the days when she forced herself not just to meet every deadline, but to beat every deadline. Now she says to everyone, herself included, "It will all get done, it will all get done," twice for emphasis. Jessica does not doubt that her bumpy road with its happy ending to motherhood has made her a more grateful and kinder person, and a more sensitive, perceptive, and trusting leader. ❖

"Creating jobs through great products. That's what keeps me passionate."

—Yve-Car Momperousse
Founder and CEO, Kreyol Essence
(Episode 171)

There are many layers to Yve-Car Momperousse's backstory and her founding of Kreyol Essence. It begins with the message she had internalized somewhere in her Haitian-American upbringing that for women, especially women of color, you are simply more attractive if your hair is straight. (We won't go into all the ramifications of that awful message to women, but for Yve-Car, it was deeply ingrained.) In her words: "What society had taught me years on end is that if you want to look your best . . . straighten your hair."

So when she decided to actively search for a husband, she asked her stylist to straighten her big Afro for a particular event. There's good news and bad news in the aftermath of this treatment. The good news is that she found her husband, who is the COO and co-founder of the company, as well as her emotional rock. The bad news is that after that treatment, her hair all fell out. She described what happened next: "Like any good millennial, the first thing I did was cry. And then the next thing I did was call my mom." She asked about the oil she remembered her mother using on her hair to straighten and nourish it when she was a child. It was Haitian black castor oil. When it worked its healing magic on the adult Yve-Car, as it always had, mother and daughter joked together that they should start selling it since they couldn't find the Haitian-cultivated product in the US. Then the joke turned serious, and a business was born.

This amazing elixir became the cornerstone of Kreyol Essence, not only for its efficacy. As a small island nation that doesn't produce much, Haiti has to import virtually everything it needs, which helps to explain why it is the poorest country in the Western Hemisphere. The local supply chain created by Kreyol Essence supports hundreds of jobs for farmers and producers, many of them women, and has had a tangible impact on the country's economy. Featured on *Shark Tank*, the "magic" oil is now available at Ulta Beauty, Whole Foods, JC Penney, and many more stores across the United States.

In Haiti, a young woman running a multi-million-dollar business is a rarity. Yve-Car wryly recalls meeting with farmers and producers on the ground in Haiti and how the men would walk right by her to ask other men on her team for guidance or decisions on production. They were shocked when they were told to go talk to the lovely young woman who was the boss. Lessons were learned all around.

Yve-Car sums up her mission-driven success and what it means to her, beyond the financial rewards: "In addition to offering great beauty products, we can help to change an entire country and create a blueprint that people can follow for poverty alleviation around the world." Kreyol Essence and its thoughtful, insightful leader prove that you can run a profitable business and fulfill a social mission at the same time. ❖

"Seeing the lines wrapping around the corner at food banks is heart-wrenching."

—Alicia Grande
Founder and CEO, Grande Cosmetics
(Episode 155)

Long, beautiful eyelashes may not be the key to life, but to Alicia Grande, they have a real purpose that's about more than glamour and vanity. In a pandemic-centric, mostly masked world, our eyes have been doing a lot of talking for us. Alicia wanted to do whatever she could to support eyes that speak beautifully.

Her business started with just one product created by a doctor and scientist team—a serum that enhances and thickens natural lashes. Unlike many lash products, this one delivers on its promise. From a tiny trade show booth tucked away in a corner, Alicia gave out samples and encouraged people to use them. Just about everyone who did eventually placed an order because the serum really works. The company has since grown, now offering mascaras, products for brows, lips, and more, but the lash serum remains the star. Perhaps because of her eye-focused product line, her e-comm business has surged during the pandemic when many beauty brands were just hunkering down and hoping to survive. This underscores for her what she knows: expressive eyes are powerful.

As the pandemic took hold in the spring of 2020, Alicia got busy with two philanthropic projects. Seeing the number of people relying on food banks broke her heart, so she started a program called Beauty from the Heart. Through it, the company offers product discounts and donates the discounted amount to Feeding America, raising over $200,000 for its network of three hundred food banks across the country. Additionally, she started a campaign to donate products directly to essential workers. Having grown up with very little, this self-made entrepreneur is delighted to be able to give back, especially in the era of COVID-19 when the need is so great. In her words, "We've been really fortunate, and I'm just so happy that I could give back at this horrible time." She hopes to inspire others to do the same. ❖

"Failure is not scary. Success is scary.
Nobody is prepared for it."

—Courtney and Tye Caldwell
Co-founders, ShearShare
(Episode 90)

Partners in everything—marriage, parenting, business—Courtney and Tye Caldwell are innovators. They met when Courtney was a client in Tye's hair salon with a different stylist. He finagled a way to meet her, and their amazing partnership was born.

Taking advantage of the booming gig economy, ShearShare is an app that matches stylists looking for by-the-day chair rentals with salons that have empty chairs, vetting all the participants to ensure a seamless and secure experience. The idea was an accident, its seed sown when Tye got a call from an out-of-town stylist. She had local clients who needed her for a big event, but since she was no longer affiliated with a salon, she asked if he had an available chair she could rent just for the day. At first, they thought it was crazy; the industry just didn't work that way. But as they thought about it, they saw its potential, with more stylists moving around and more salons closing. So they tried it. Then this same stylist asked them if they knew of chairs for rent by the day in other cities. The word spread. And they were off. For three years, they manually matched stylists and chairs, calling upon their expansive and expanding network to vet all the participants. Then they realized there was a better way and developed the app, jokingly yet accurately referred to as "Hairbnb."

Mentoring has been a constant theme in Tye's life. He recalled how, in high school, he would help one of his favorite lower-school teachers grade papers after school and got to know some of her students, eventually becoming a student, instructor. He acknowledges his natural leadership skills and has always wanted to use those skills to help others. ShearShare is a way of doing that, as he and Courtney play matchmakers between stylists without fixed homes and salons that are trying to fill their chairs to pay the rent. As the brick-and-mortar salon industry has evolved and stylists seek more flexibility, the business has found its footing, now operating in 433 cities and 11 countries. It has been a win-win.

This remarkable couple delights in supporting the industry they love, focusing on the community, not the competition. Tye expressed how it saddens them when they get calls from salon owners who are closing up shop. "We just cringe when we hear that. We got tired of seeing our friends close down." Through ShearShare, they can help. They shared the challenges along the way, Courtney lovingly summing it up: "Every day, this man grabs my hand and says, 'Let's run and jump off this cliff.' I'm like, 'Okay, let's do it!'"

Grateful for each other and joyful in their work, Tye and Courtney cherish the salon community and the opportunity to support it, even on those tear-your-hair-out days. And they certainly recognize the challenges that come with success. But in the end, they are mentors *par excellence.* ❖

> *"It's as much a passion about the makeup as it is about cultivating and mentoring other women."*
>
> —Wende Zomnir
> Founding partner, Urban Decay Cosmetics
> (Episode 142)

The idea behind Urban Decay is nothing less than the democratization of beauty. When Wende Zomnir was concepting the makeup line over twenty-five years ago, she thought about where beauty trends come from and who was choosing the "it" lipstick shade each season. She had a pretty good idea it was some executive (probably a man) in some corporate office tower, studying some spreadsheet rather than focusing on what women might actually want. Wende and her partner decided that one size—or color—definitely does not fit all. Most of us aren't pretty enough, tall enough, skinny enough, or *anything* enough to meet some idealized standard of what women "should" look like. Urban Decay was born to transform makeup from bland and safe to edgy and disruptive, freeing women from convention along the way.

From day one, a huge part of Wende's mission has been to support and inspire women, both the women she sells to and the women she works with. The Urban Decay journey started with a serendipitous call with a legendary woman from big tech—a rarity twenty-five years ago. This super-smart entrepreneur was also a makeup junkie who wanted to shake up the beauty industry. Then just twenty-seven and quite green, Wende didn't know what to expect, but her partner, having made it big in a man's world, was loaded with confidence and passed it on to Wende. It turned out to be an amazing partnership that underscores why Wende feels so strongly about paying it forward by mentoring women as she was mentored.

For Wende, what she sells and the way she runs her business are inextricably linked, with a company culture that's inclusive and supportive of her team in the same way that their products are making beauty more open and less dictatorial. She talks about how, in Urban Decay's infancy, there was no Sephora with its hundreds of brands, and no social media with its armies of influencers. But gradually, women began to have more choices than just the mega brands decreeing the look of the moment. They could finally see images of people who looked like them, not just perfect, size-two models in glossy magazines. Liberation! In Wende's words, "It just fueled itself. It really turned the industry around."

That freedom to choose, and the belief that no one should tell anyone else how they should look, are the essence of the beauty revolution that is Urban Decay. Beyond selling products, Wende takes joy in sharing her story and encouraging everyone to be true to who they are and how they want to present themselves to the world. As she works to empower the women around her, she is doing the same for herself. ❖

MY "MORE"

When I started the *Where Brains Meet Beauty* podcast five years ago, my purpose was to explore the backstories of those I had met in the beauty and wellness industries, to learn about their beginnings, their paths, their challenges, and where they were headed on a personal level. I wanted to humanize the industry and give leaders a chance to share, vent, or just talk about their own experiences in a safe space with someone who had faced some of the same challenges they had. It was not intended as a marketing tool or a publicity opportunity, just members of a community sharing stories. What I didn't know then was how much more it would become, growing into a valuable resource for our guests, their colleagues, their customers, and every listener, whether part of our industry or not. There are many universal messages throughout our more than two hundred episodes. Over and over, we receive feedback on how a particular conversation resonated with a listener, gave someone the confidence to raise a sensitive issue with their boss, maybe gave a would-be entrepreneur a needed nudge. Teaching and mentorship themes are well represented, and it gives me joy to know that these discussions have had such far-reaching ripples.

Philanthropy runs deep in our industry, and Base Beauty is no exception. I feel blessed to be able to contribute my time and resources to support organizations I believe in, including the Skin of Color Society, and serving on the board of Girls Helping Girls. Period.

I am often asked about the origins of the name *Where Brains Meet Beauty*. It started as a tagline for our agency, Base Beauty, cleverly combatting the notion that beauty was frivolous and fluffy, and that brains and beauty could not coexist. Everything we do as an agency and the podcast speaks to what happens when brilliant minds use their brains to support our industry. It has become the perfect name for the podcast and its purpose. ❖

Lesson Learned

Paying it forward and paying it back are two sides of the same coin. I take my role as teacher and mentor to my team very seriously and celebrate their growth. I am grateful for everyone who did the same for me, even those who taught me how not to behave. I will always share my success, both within Base Beauty and with the world at large. ❖

SOUND BITES

Lean on me.

There's room for lots of businesses to succeed.

Pay it forward.

It definitely takes a village.

Trust is the essence of leadership.

There should be no "shoulds" in beauty.

FOOD FOR THOUGHT

➤ Whatever community you are part of, how have you called on your colleagues (or your competitors) for help with common challenges?

➤ Who was your most significant mentor? Does that person know how meaningful they were to you?

➤ Who have you mentored that you are most proud of having helped to grow? Are there additional ways you can be generous with your expertise to help someone else grow in their career?

8

BEING THE BOSS

Brains & Beauty-ism #8
**It's not just about the goop in the jar.
It's about relationships.**

E very guest on *Where Brains Meet Beauty* is a leader. Some lead mega-corporations or departments within mega-corporations. Some lead tiny, or once-tiny, start-ups launched at their kitchen tables and eventually sold to mega-corporations. Some lead huge teams. Some are one-(wo)man bands, consultants, influencers, bloggers, or some combination. Our roster of over two hundred guests represents a wide array of leadership styles and situations. But the common thread is that each guest wanted to run the show, whatever size that show turned out to be. Whether the catalyst was a childhood dream, an innovative concept, a random opportunity, or just wanting to call the shots, each leader summoned the courage and the confidence to put it all on the line, many starting without much of either.

There's another thread that weaves throughout these stories of leadership, one that reaches beyond the goal of being in charge and selling a lot of stuff. That's the desire to teach and inspire those who work for them and with them. In many instances, as already mentioned, discovering and mentoring talent was as strong a motivator as the product, the power, the freedom, or the financial reward in defining their career path. These are folks who care about other folks and want to help everyone in their orbits succeed. Over and over, as guests shared their views on leadership and their interactions with their teams, I was impressed and moved by their "whys." It all comes down to relationships.

I'm sure there are those in many industries who lead according to a people-centric ethos, but I believe that the beauty world has more than its fair share of such generous souls. I think that's because our work is about helping people to look their best, feel their best, keep their skin healthy, and have confidence in how they present themselves to the world. That is no small mission, and it takes passion and kindness to pursue it. ❖

> *"I've created an environment where people leave the office at a normal hour and have a life."*
>
> —Sarah Kugelman
> CEO and founder, skyn ICELAND
> (Episode 143)

As recently as 2005, the connection between the stress in our lives and the health of our skin was still a new concept. Sarah Kugelman was one of the first to recognize it and address it. Sarah's is a fascinating story. Holding major corporate jobs in beauty, the entrepreneur in her kept poking out its head, even though she tried several times to put that genie back in the bottle. Because she's a creative thinker, she could not ignore the ideas that kept popping into her head. She was destined to bounce around a bit; running her own business was inevitable.

Her zigzag trajectory (simplified) goes something like this:
- Running the fragrance division at Banana Republic
- Launching Gloss.com, a multi-brand, prestige beauty website (a concept unheard of at the time)
- Selling Gloss.com to Estée Lauder
- Returning to a high-stress corporate job with long hours and lots of travel
- Teetering on the edge of burnout, ultimately landing in the hospital
- Hearing the wake-up call
- Creating a skincare line targeting the effects of stress on skin

- Dialing down the stress in her life, still working hard but on her own terms

The clean, vegan, healthy skincare line Sarah founded, skyn ICELAND, is specifically formulated to address the effects of stress on skin. But Sarah also explores the causes of the deep stress that affects overall wellness: balancing work and family (more intense for women); striving for perfection (also more intense for women); and the pressure to work long hours, and even jeopardize your health in many corporations to show your devotion to your job. She's growing skyn ICELAND beyond just a skincare line, into a resource for health, wellness, and women's empowerment.

From the beginning, Sarah has been committed to creating a business culture that works for her team. She remembers corporate life where people often had to maneuver or even be a little deceitful just to find time for a doctor's appointment. That environment contributed to the high-stress level, so she's having none of that with skyn ICELAND. She describes what's important to her as a leader: "My team is dedicated and loyal to me because I respect them and give them the freedom to have a life. They're in charge of their schedules, their lives, and their work, and they're accountable for getting it done."

Sarah's leadership style is perfectly in sync with the mission of her products. Ideally, if no one had any stress at work or in life, they might not need stress-addressing skincare. But since that's not the case, Sarah is committed to solving stress on skin and in her workplace. For her, they are two sides of the same coin.

Sarah shared a meaningful story about a make-or-break moment early on. Skyn ICELAND was about ten days away from being out of money and closing the doors. Sarah had just had a baby and was on maternity leave—at least, an entrepreneur's version of maternity leave. Skyn ICELAND had been nominated for the *Women's Wear Daily* Indie Beauty Award. She wasn't even planning to attend the awards luncheon, certain there was no reason to, but her husband and mother told her she had to go. So she went. And she won. And that award sealed the deal for an investor who had been on the fence. She saw that award as "a sign that I needed to keep doing this." Now on the board of the Tufts Entrepreneurship Center, helping to create opportunities for aspiring women entrepreneurs, she often shares this anecdote with her advisees, telling them to "look for the signs that are telling you to keep going." ❖

"It's about helping people to get the best out of themselves. That's where the fun happens."

—Emily Culp
CEO, Cover FX
(Episode 141)

Fun is not a word often heard in the C-suite. Except in Emily Culp's C-suite. In leading clean, vegan makeup line Cover FX, she cherishes being able to mentor and empower people, helping them become the best versions of themselves professionally. In describing her leadership style, she explains why she never, ever looks at emails during the day, saving them for her commute so she can be present for her team. "It's actually about connecting with the people who work with you . . . inspiring them, helping them resolve things together. That's actually where you get your team to do amazing things." And that's the fun.

While she's passionate about the brand, which is perfectly aligned with her values of inclusivity and diversity, Emily was never a hardcore beauty junkie and didn't have her eye on a top leadership role. Her rise to the C-suite happened organically. She had been at Keds, where she had been recruited to put together the marketing plan for the iconic footwear brand's centennial—a marketer's dream job. As key players left, she kept climbing. Then Cover FX came calling, and she embraced the opportunity to guide another iconic brand while building in the values that are meaningful for her.

In talking to Emily about her work, she doesn't mention profits or market share or other financial markers. She believes that if you focus on your people, the metrics will follow. The essence of her job is creating a corporate culture that's safe and supportive and gives people room to grow. She leads with respect, transparency, flexibility, integrity, and humility. Yes, humility, another word rarely heard in the C-suite.

Part of executing these policies is how she manages time, from color-coded Post-its with daily goals, to staying away from her computer when she's in her office, to sacrosanct dinnertime with her kids. By sticking to her regimens, she can be truly present for her team at work and for her family at home, which keeps things humming in both places without distractions. It's not a perfect system, but it mostly works.

Describing herself as "insanely curious," Emily always reminds herself why she's doing what she's doing. She thinks we all need to focus on what we love about our work, especially on those tear-your-hair-out days. With a unique perspective from both inside and outside the beauty world, she's the kind of boss that everyone would want to work for, who illustrates that it's possible to put people first and still stay on top. ❖

*"You have to give people the opportunity
to make mistakes, grow, and learn."*

—Rita Hazan

Celebrity colorist and owner, Rita Hazan Salon
(Episode 102)

There's a wise quote on leadership from Steve Jobs: "It doesn't make sense to hire smart people and then tell them what to do; we hire smart people so they can tell us what to do." These words could have been said by Rita Hazan, who has thought a lot about what it means to lead. She believes you hire the right people, train them well, then leave them alone so they can do their jobs. She knows how difficult it is, especially for founders, to delegate and trust and keep from hovering, but she knows it's the only way to let your team and your business grow.

Running a three-pronged hair care business—a salon, a product line, and a celebrity division—means she's always on. But Rita has developed a couple of ways to manage the endless workload. One of these is a habit of always being in the moment, focusing on one task at a time, so she doesn't get distracted thinking about everything on her to-do list. She's always aware of the big picture, but she doesn't let it overwhelm her. Another coping skill is walking away. As she says, "If I can't stop and reboot my brain, I can't see the path. So I walk away, come back in the room, and then see everything with a clean, clear perspective." She views that ability to gain perspective as a crucial quality in an effective leader.

Further illustrating this need to walk away, Rita is the rare entrepreneur who actually takes vacations—real vacations. She turns off her phone, disconnects from social media, and luxuriates in time away from everything. Her comfort in being able to do this goes back to her team. She figures, even if a few mistakes are made in her absence, or a few decisions are made that she would have decided differently, her business won't be completely destroyed in a week or two. "I'm very particular about the people I hire. If you have to stay on top of your people, then you didn't hire the right people."

Rita has developed a lot of wisdom on letting go so your business can grow. Particularly in a personal service business, it's all about the people around you. She is proud of her skill at finding talent that's the right fit for her multi ventures, and then trusting them to do their jobs. She sums it up, "You can't be the smartest person in the room all the time. . . . You have to listen." ❖

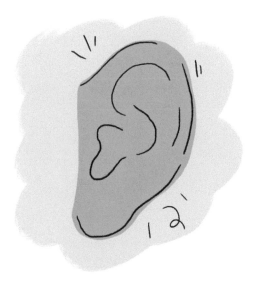

"All my opportunities are because of people."

—Allison Slater Ray
President, Memebox
(Episode 130)

The soul of an entrepreneur and the experience of a corporate executive coexist in Allison Slater Ray, giving her a rare perspective that explains her reputation as one of the best brand builders in the business. With a deep background, from the retail side at Sephora and the brand side at IT Cosmetics and Memebox, among other gigs, Allison has seen it all. She knows how to distinguish those brands that want to ride a trendy wave and make a quick buck from those with a mission and a passion to create a legacy brand with staying power. No surprise that Allison has used her talents and vision to help put more than one beauty brand on the map. Part of her unique ability is that even though she has extensive corporate experience, she always keeps her entrepreneur's viewpoint, knowing what it takes to launch, grow, and maintain a brand.

Allison attributes her success to a combination of timing, luck, generous mentors, and relentless networking, plus lots of hard work. Her journey to the top of the beauty ladder began with a "gift" job at advertising agency DDB—she walked in and was assigned to the glamorous Chanel account when more senior colleagues were selling toilet paper and dog food. The next stop was Sephora in its early days as a brand incubator, a role that touched the entrepreneur within her as she helped baby brands find their footing. Allison views her years at Sephora as a time of paying it forward; those who mentored her early in her career made it possible for her to serve as a mentor to developing brands—an opportunity she treasures.

At every step, from her move to IT Cosmetics to taking the reins at the Memebox group of Korean makeup and skincare brands, Allison never forgets those who encouraged, supported, nudged, and advised her through all the jobs and all the years. She speaks of the importance of having someone outside of your professional life for venting and bouncing around ideas, either a spouse, a friend, or a parent. No discussion of her journey is complete without her shout-out to her mother, the source of many of the tools in Allison's toolbox. A strong, get-it-done woman, Allison describes her mom as "politely aggressive." Allison inherited this quality, although she thinks of herself as too polite and not aggressive enough at times. But as she carries on the attitude she was raised with, she's deeply grateful to those who have been there for her along the way. This beauty leader illustrates that leadership is really about recognizing and supporting those around you, and helping everyone climb the ladder together. ❖

"Remember, it's your passion, but it's their job."

—Lisa Price
Founder, Carol's Daughter
(Episode 87)

In beauty, it's always about what's new and what's next. Lots of brands start out strong, but many don't make it past the five-year mark. Celebrating a brand's twenty-five year anniversary is rarer still. Carol's Daughter is a hair care line built on clean, premium ingredients, innovative formulas, and honest, no-hype marketing. Lisa Price started Carol's Daughter in her Brooklyn kitchen in 1993, and sold it to L'Oreal twenty-five years later. The brand is still going strong, as is its founder.

Lisa's perspective on her business's trajectory is both micro and macro, from the detail-packed grind at the beginning, to a bird's-eye view now that she is no longer involved in every decision. She talks about the early days when it took her a while to grasp that those working for her, dedicated as they were, happily headed for the door at 5:00 p.m. At first, she couldn't understand why no one else ate, slept, and breathed the business the way she did (a founder's attitude that's not unusual, just unreasonable). Birthing a business is like being a parent—no one will ever love your child as you do, and no one will ever share the intensity of a founder's passion.

Understanding that line between the owner/founder/nurturer-in-chief and the employees did not dampen Lisa's desire to help her team learn and grow. She thinks she has a special gift for recognizing talented people and helping them develop as professionals. Lisa reflects on her leadership style: "I believe I attract people who come and work and learn and give and share, but then take what they need and fly away." Like a proud mama bird, she cheers for them when they spread their wings and leave the nest. Then she nurtures the fledglings still with her in the same way.

Lisa also spoke about the inevitable self-doubts in leading a company, especially if you've never done it before. Even when business was good, she still struggled sometimes with feeling competent and confident. She recalls how she learned to handle stressful negotiations with big-time investors and potential buyers, often by finding people to talk to who had nothing to do with the business. These days, even though the stress is less, she still calls upon some coping skills she has developed, such as stepping way back, slowing way down, breathing deeply, and listening to a playlist she created that calms and inspires her. Knowing that challenges are common in growing a business, she advises others to identify their release valves and remember to use them. For Lisa, this helps her enjoy the ride. ✤

> *"I wanted to create a culture where people could thrive, have job satisfaction, and know that they were cared for."*
>
> —Amy Shecter
> CEO, Glamsquad
> (Episode 118)

Amy Shecter understood personal branding before there was such a thing. She just thought of it as being smart and strategic in planning her career path, always seeking positions that would teach her a new business skill. She had her eye on the C-suite early on, but she wanted to make sure she was ready when the opportunity presented itself. Having spent years in fashion, building an impressive resume—Bloomingdale's, Lady Foot Locker, Diesel, Donna Karan, Cole Haan, Tory Burch—she learned crucial lessons in leadership at every turn, from leading and from being led.

Leadership for Amy is about finding the right balance between driving the train (guiding the day-to-day), laying down the tracks (the future), and fixing the engine (problem-solving). She has learned as CEO that she needs to take the 360-helicopter view for strategy, planning, communication, and finance while also being able to swoop in with hands-on help when needed. She thinks she's struck that balance at Glamsquad.

And yet, while spending as much time as possible looking at the big picture, Amy is fiercely committed to working closely with her team to help them develop as professionals. She has created a highly collaborative environment at Glamsquad where people work together and learn from each other. But she goes way beyond that, offering ongoing professional coaching to whoever wants it, whatever their level; scheduling team meetings with guest speakers; and implementing a series of training programs to let people in one area of the business gain exposure to other areas.

Always sensitive to people's day-to-day lives, Amy has also implemented adaptive scheduling so that people can take their kids to school or schedule a doctor's appointment without stressing about it. Flexibility is the key, for both her permanent staff and the network of professionals who provide the Glamsquad services. She sums up her approach: "We're a modern-day beauty brand with a modern-day approach to business."

Not every CEO puts "professional development" near the top of their job description list as Amy does. By doing so, she's creating a capable, fulfilled, and loyal team that brings her as much personal gratification as it does them. ❖

MY LEADERSHIP

I've touched on many aspects of leadership in these pages—mentoring, listening, adapting, supporting. But let me share some further thoughts on why I wanted to start my own business, and why I think I am an effective leader.

After all my jobs—sometimes working for good people, sometimes for awful people—I had learned a lot about what makes a good leader and what makes a terrible one. As someone who suffered from crippling self-doubt for most of my early career, I knew all too well what it was like not to have a sense of agency. When I started my business, it was with the personal goal of leading my own life as a mother and a human in a way that felt right for me. I wasn't going to let an employer's rules determine what kind of mom I would be. I wanted control over my schedule. I wanted a team that I could trust to take over when needed so that I could go on vacation once in a while, attend a school play, or stay home with a sick child without everything in the business grinding to a halt.

Along with the goal of choice, I knew that starting my own business would allow me to merge my values and my work, structuring a business built on respect, kindness, and empathy, as well as prosperity. Lofty goals, for sure, but I am proud to say that I think we have achieved them at Base Beauty. I have not done it alone. The remarkable people who work with me put these values into practice every day. I will take credit for having a good "nose" for talented people who care about the culture of their workplace, not just their paycheck. And while you often don't have as much control as you would like, it's essential to realize that you can't—and shouldn't—try to control everything. Now, when I give up control by delegating or when twelve projects walk in the door at once, and we're all working at warp speed, I can meet the challenges in a way that's consistent with Base Beauty's core values.

Over the years, I've recognized that one of my talents as a leader is my ability to see things ten steps ahead. This is incredibly useful in everything from executing a single project on the micro level to planning business growth on the macro level. It's not something I studied; it's just part of how I observe the world, and I am grateful for this gift. This instinct has served me well and contributes to my overall goal of having choices. I look at the forks in the road and choose which one will lead to the place I want the business to be. Maybe every leader does that; perhaps that's what defines effective leadership. It is a valuable quality that helps Base Beauty keep evolving and adapting along with the marketplace so we can always offer our clients fresh, relevant solutions. ❖

Lesson Learned

You can't control everything, but you can create a responsive culture that gives you choices, and choices give you freedom. Keep evolving because when you're stagnant, you run out of options. ❖

SOUND BITES

Remember why you're doing what you're doing.

**Sometimes you have to unplug the cords
or turn off the screens.**

Don't say yes to everything.

Let go so you can grow.

Leadership is about teaching and supporting.

Leadership is about people.

FOOD FOR THOUGHT

➤ When and how did you discover that you could lead in business, either starting your own, running a department within a larger company, or simply being the boss of your own work?

➤ What was your strongest motivation for choosing to be a leader?

➤ How did your leadership style evolve? How did you define the type of leader you wanted to be?

9

REFLECTIONS ON THE JOURNEY

Brains & Beauty-ism #9
It takes all you can give—and then it takes more.

Our roster of guests on *Where Brains Meet Beauty* runs the gamut from seasoned C-suite executives to just-starting-out novices. But it's heavily weighted with entrepreneurs. Perhaps that's because of the nature of the beauty industry, where barriers to entry are not always that steep, and a business can be launched with just one innovative product, so lots of people try. It might also be attributed to the stories I choose to spotlight—I'm drawn like a magnet to pioneering ideas and to founders who are passionate and authentic and find the fun in the struggle.

I believe that the business world—maybe the rest of the world, too—is divided into those who have that entrepreneurial, work-for-myself itch, and those who don't. There's something in the DNA of the independents that sets us apart and motivates us to jump off the entrepreneurial cliff. Many people

139

work hard, but entrepreneurs work doubly or triply hard, usually without much help or any safety net at the beginning—a beginning that might last for years. We hustle and sweat, we worry and doubt, yet we constantly find creative ways to face the challenges and keep on going.

Here are seven short stories of guts and glory—random observations, in their own words—on the great adventure of running a business. Five of them are from founders, one is from an owner, and one focuses on an aspiring journalist who set her sights and relentlessly pursued her target writing job. They know what it takes. Brave souls, all. ❖

"Give yourself grace because this s*** is hard."

—Beatrice Dixon
CEO and co-founder, The Honey Pot Company
(Episode 175)

Like many entrepreneurs, Beatrice Dixon launched The Honey Pot Company, a line of herb-based feminine care products, to solve a personal need, specifically chronic bacterial vaginosis. She drew on her background in pharmacy and her work in wellness, plus a formula that came to her—wait for it—in a dream where she was visited by her long-deceased grandmother, who handed her a list of ingredients. It sounds preposterous, but the formula she created with this otherworldly guidance worked and planted the seed for her product line, now in Target and every major mass drugstore and supermarket. (Next time you think dreams aren't meaningful, remember Beatrice's.)

In her words: "It takes time, it takes effort, it takes thick skin, it takes love, it takes patience . . . it takes listening, and it takes intuition." ❖

"I never look at things as being stressful and scary. I look at them as a challenge and an adventure."

—Rea Ann Silva
Founder and CEO, Beauty Blender
(Episode 139)

It was a long road from Rea Ann Silva's work as the always-avoided department store perfume spritzer to her thriving career as a union makeup artist on film and TV sets. Even so, when she arrived at what she thought was her dream job, she still wanted more. Her "more" evolved directly from her work. Frustrated by the angled edges of the only makeup sponges available, which left tiny ridges and streaks picked up by the newest HD cameras, she grabbed scissors and snipped the edges to soften the sponges' contours, enabling a totally smooth application. Other makeup artists began asking her to snip sponges for them. "Aha," she thought, "here's a need and an opportunity." Her little rounded sponges turned out to be game-changing, finding a following and becoming the springboard for a flourishing beauty business.

In her words: "I have to take risks, but I look at them as opportunities to achieve my goals. If one of them doesn't work out, then guess what? I learned a lesson, but I don't let that fear or anxiety control the way I behave." ❖

> *"Make sure you're not just doing it for the money."*
>
> —Marcia Kilgore
> Founder, Beauty Pie, Bliss Spa, Soap & Glory, FitFlop
> (Episode 61)

Serial entrepreneur Marcia Kilgore has a string of hits to her credit—Bliss Beauty, FitFlop, Soap and Glory, and now Beauty Pie. The common thread is that each business was game-changing in its way, launched by Marcia to rethink outdated ways of doing things. With Beauty Pie, she is democratizing beauty by offering carefully curated, lab-direct products through a membership program, letting customers experiment with new products without making huge investments. Products are more accessible and of higher quality, lab margins are better, and Beauty Pie's profits are healthy but not insane. It's a win-win-win and another feather in Marcia's impressive cap. You can imagine all the wisdom she has acquired through each of her ventures—wisdom that she happily shares.

In her words: "You don't have to be this goddess of 'I know everything.' The best thing I've ever done is bring people in who are better than me to question me. People are very happy to give their opinions. You can take it or leave it, but boy, it's eye-opening when you listen." ❖

"You have to slowly but surely tell yourself that you're worthy and that you belong, and you eventually have to believe it."

—Essence Gant
Beauty Director, BuzzFeed
(Episode 108)

Essence Gant did not have a roadmap to reach her dream job—she didn't even know what that job was except that it would lie somewhere at the intersection of entertainment, media, and beauty. She knew she loved to write, and had an idea she was pretty good at it. So when an established blogger and reality TV writer offered her an unpaid internship—asking her to cover New York Fashion Week as her first assignment—she jumped at it, feeling a little daunted, but plowing ahead anyway. (A supportive chance meeting with stylist and costume designer June Ambrose at one of the shows gave her the confidence boost she needed.) With some helpful writing hints along the way, one thing led to another and another and then to BuzzFeed. Even once there, it took her a while to shed the "imposter syndrome" and feel that she was worthy of the opportunity. But she finally did, and loves the chance to introduce beauty brands to the BuzzFeed audience. Her goal at BuzzFeed is to continue to pay it forward and show other girls who look like her that they can succeed at anything.

In her words: "[That first job] pushed me so far out of my comfort zone and tested every bit of patience, strength, and resourcefulness that I had. . . . I know that it's given me what I needed to succeed, so I don't regret it. But it was very hard." ❖

"It's about letting go of all of that negative energy and welcoming what really serves you."

—Diana Briceno
CEO, No B.S. Skincare
(Episode 152)

A practical sort, Diana Briceno followed the family tradition and studied engineering. One day, she took a random test for an internship at a mystery company recruiting on her college campus. That company turned out to be Procter & Gamble, and the internship she was offered was in marketing. She wasn't quite sure how all the math, physics, and chemistry would come into play, but she thought maybe the universe had a plan for her, so she went with it. After eight exciting and expansive years in the P&G prestige division, she tired of the massive, multilayered, ultra-compartmentalized corporation. That's when the little entrepreneurial voice in her head began to grow louder and louder, and she started work on her skincare brand, disruptive in name and in philosophy.

On first hearing, the name sounds like just a clever attention-grabber, but it stands for much more. The meaning behind the name (no bull**** or no bad stuff, whichever you prefer) starts with the ingredients—definitely no bad stuff there—but extends beyond the products to no-hype marketing, no false promises, no pushing women to look a certain way. Diana and her team have a B.S. meter in everything they do, constantly questioning and jettisoning any idea or plan that isn't 100 percent authentic. She's proud to be offering clean, quality products, and to lead a company that practices what it preaches, with no room for any B.S.

In her words: "A lot of my work as an entrepreneur and as the CEO is to get rid of stuff that doesn't really add value. And I guess that the test of this is, 'Is this a bit B.S.-y, or is it really awesome?' That always helps because the moment we think it, we just don't do it and move on." ✤

"If you do what you love, you can be successful."
—Stephanie Morimoto
Owner and CEO, Asutra
(Episode 197)

It took Stephanie Morimoto a few tries to figure out what she wanted to do with her professional life. Starting out to be an ophthalmologist like her adored grandfather, a year of college chemistry convinced her that dream was not the right one. Her first job out of college was teaching English in Hiroshima, Japan—an incredible experience that showed her the inequities in education and the value of a quality education. Her entrepreneurial side was sparked by her work at the consulting firm McKinsey, as she learned about running a big company and decided that was not for her either. But seeds were sown, and values were developing around working with products she believed in and creating good jobs in communities where they were needed. She knew she was not wired to start a business from scratch, but thought that she could grow a business that was on its way. Such an opportunity crossed her path—the wellness company Asutra, whose products happened to be in Stephanie's medicine cabinet because she loved them. Talk about serendipity! She bought the company and set about building a brand story from a collection of great but disconnected products. Moving the business to her home city of Chicago, she created good jobs and opportunities along the way.

In her words: "It took a lot of reflection, therapy, really thinking about and feeling who do I want to be in this world, and what's the impact I want to have? And recognizing that failing along the way is going to be part of that journey, and that's okay." ❖

"Find your people. Your people are out there."

—Sara Happ

Founder and CEO, Sara Happ

(Episode 195)

Embarking on a career in on-air broadcast journalism, Sara Happ discovered during college that there were people in her journalism program who were much better suited to that career than she was. She recalls her first job at ESPN: her colleagues would spend weekends immersed in sports, watching four screens while listening to a game on the radio—she would go home and take a bubble bath filled with luxurious products. She happily realized she was "a beauty girl at heart," reading the style magazines, not the sports news. Part of that discovery was identifying her entrepreneurial side. And she had an idea for a product—a lip scrub—that didn't even exist back in 2005. She was advised to go to business school first before setting out to launch her product, advice she is glad she ignored. "I think that business school would have probably scared me out of a lot of the moves that I made." Specializing in skincare for lips, Sara has kept her brand focused on what she does best, despite others telling her that she would never be able to build a business with just lip products. Sixteen years later, it has been a joy for Sara to prove the naysayers wrong.

In her words: "Wherever you are in life, the more challenges you face, the stronger you do get. . . . Just keep betting on yourself because we are all smarter and stronger than we think we are." ❖

MY REFLECTIONS

For a long time, I thought of my life as divided into two "camps": work in one camp, and everything else—family, friends, "me" time—in the other. Separate and not always equal (see Chapter Three). It took me a long time to realize that, in terms of personal growth, it's all one journey. Every day, whether I'm growing my business, being a mom, or working out at the gym, I'm constantly evolving as a human being. The seductive challenges of entrepreneurship are actually helpful in that evolution since they are constant, and they are exhausting (as well as fun and exhilarating). There's always another hill to climb and another AFGO (see Chapter Six). Each day is a test that helps me know what I'm made of and where I need to grow. As I face each one, I try to be mindful of the progress I've made and grateful for those around me who boost my confidence along the way. ❖

Lesson Learned

I need to be a continual work in progress. I don't ever want to "arrive" at my personal goals. I have experienced the joy of approaching my life with an attitude of openness and kindness. I have learned to take some pressure off myself to be perfect, to give myself permission to change my mind, and to remember that my most important task is working on myself. ❖

SOUND BITES

Entrepreneurs are different.

Entrepreneurs love a challenge.

Entrepreneurs never quit, even when they should.

**Entrepreneurs see opportunity
where others see problems.**

**Entrepreneurs pay it forward
because they remember when.**

Entrepreneurs are different.

FOOD FOR THOUGHT

➤ What is your number one goal for personal growth?

➤ What is standing in your way of achieving it?

➤ When did you know that you had what it takes to reach your goals? How many times did you doubt or second guess yourself?

10

IN THE BEGINNING . . .

Brains & Beauty-ism #10
Dreams matter.

I n the first few years of *Where Brains Meet Beauty*, when we were recording in person in our office studio, I always had the opportunity to chat with my guests for a few minutes before each session. I loved those mini meet-and-greets, and they served as easy icebreakers for our recorded conversations since this was often the first time I met my guests in person. I might have waved to them across a crowded room at an industry event, and I always spoke with them by phone to set up the episode. But in most cases, I had never looked them in the eyes or shaken their hands until they walked into our recording studio. That pre-recording meeting was invaluable.

Once we started up again after our COVID-19 hiatus, recording remotely, I didn't have that face-to-face connection as a catalyst. We had no physical contact whatsoever. So as we tiptoed back into the work world with its pandemic protocols, I wanted a way to jumpstart each episode and recreate the energy of the live recordings. I thought it would be both fun and revealing to ask guests to think back and share what their eleven-year-old selves had thought they wanted to be when they grew up. I chose eleven as an age that was still deep in childhood, but a time when kids are developing some awareness of the adult world and its possibilities.

This question turned out to be a superb way to begin each podcast episode. It caught guests a tiny bit off guard, which resulted in delightfully spontaneous answers and paved the way for the discussions of their adult journeys. Guests told me it was cool for them to think way back—which many of them had not done in years—and to consider the part that long-ago dream had played in the big picture of their career. Very few ended up following that original path, but themes from childhood wove in and out of their lives, sometimes predictably, more often unexpectedly.

I'm still beginning each recording session with this question and still getting intriguing answers. Some have been mind-blowing. Wanting to become a ballerina or an astronaut is sort of expected from a young dreamer, but what eleven-year-old even knows what a marine biologist does, wants to run a hospital where no one gets sick, or thinks about developing a line of good-for-the-planet skincare products? Not surprisingly, those who became entrepreneurs were among the biggest dreamers, even if the business they started as an adult seems to have nothing to do with the plan from childhood. Somewhere there were seeds planted and threads connected to today.

What follows are excerpts from our podcast transcripts in our guests' own words. As you read through their answers to the question I posed to their eleven-year-old selves, consider where you thought you were headed at age eleven. You might find, as I did, that the answer speaks volumes about where each of us is today, and our continuing journeys. ❖

Jodi Katz:

When you were eleven years old, and someone asked you what you wanted to be when you grew up, what was your response?

Christine Chang, co-founder and co-CEO, Glow Recipe (Episode 193)

I would've probably said artist. I still have some of the paintings from that time, but it was just my happy place. And it was the one thing that helped me transition from where I was living, which was Louisiana, with my mom and dad. And then, as a family, we moved all together back to Korea. And so, with the language barrier, I was going through a tough transition at school. It's a much tougher academic environment in Korea as well. And I feel like art was that one medium where it just translated wherever I was.

Sarah Lee, co-founder and co-CEO, Glow Recipe (Episode 193)

Pianist. I've actually been learning to play the piano since the age of five. And I fell in love with music, and it started with my mom's passion. She wanted her daughter to be a great pianist, and it was great because I was able to learn to read the notes at an early age. . . . By the time we went to school, I kind of knew everything in music class that they taught, which was really awesome. But also, I really enjoyed playing the piano. And so, I asked my mom to continue the piano lessons for years and years. Even when we, as a family, moved to Hong Kong—my dad was an ex-pat there—and the curriculum of learning piano completely shifted, I still was able to continue learning piano. And I just really enjoyed composing music as well. . . . So that was my dream for actually a very long time.

Anisa Telwar Kaicker, founder and CEO, Anisa International, Inc. (Episode 172)

I thought it would be amazing to be a pediatrician, that I would want to go into the medical field. . . . I loved my pediatrician. He was the best. He was so helpful and sweet and kind and smart. I thought that's what I would want to do. I think until I was about twelve, when I realized what would be involved to get to having a fun office with toys and giving lollipops, that there was a lot of work and a lot of blood involved, and all kinds of other things. I just knew that wasn't going to be my thing.

FACING THE SEDUCTION OF SUCCESS

Alissa Sasso, manager of consumer health, EDF+Business, Environmental Defense Fund (Episode 184)

At eleven years old, I probably would have said marine biologist. So I already had an interest in the environment, but very focused on the ocean. . . . I was lucky to be able to travel a bit with my parents and my family. And I remember snorkeling when I was pretty young, and my dad and I saw some coral reef fish caught in cages. . . . I remember we went in and let them out. And that was sort of a jumping-off point for my dad to teach me a bit about reefs. . . . Even then, I think we were starting to see some damage to reefs from climate change. So I started pretty young. I was lucky to be exposed to that sort of environment and to have a dad who was interested in teaching me about it. . . . It sparked my interest in what was happening in the world around me.

Jess Weiner, CEO and founder, Talk To Jess (Episode 168)

I wanted to be a lizard trainer. I grew up in Miami and I really thought, somehow, I would be the owner of a lizard circus one day. I still think it could be a thing.

Jenna Owens, founder, Fitish CBD Skincare (Episode 188)

I would have said, well, at the time, I was a super tomboy playing soccer, so I really idolized the Mia Hamms and that sort of thing. I loved scary shows, criminal psychology. I probably would have tried to make a career out of one of those two things, and now I'm doing neither.

IN THE BEGINNING . . .

Maria Hatzistefanis, CEO and founder, The Rodial Group (Episode 163)

I always wanted to be an editor of a magazine. Since I was very young, I would buy magazines like *Vogue* and *Elle* and *Harper's*, and I was obsessed with the world of beauty and fashion and glamour. And I was born and raised on this tiny island where everything was really basic. This was my escape, reading those magazines and thinking that one day I would be in a different place. And I always imagined that I would run a magazine.

Amy Gordinier, founder and CEO, Skinfix (Episode 187)

I definitely wanted to be a professional athlete. And I played volleyball, so I guess, a volleyball player. But I just loved sports, and the idea of being able to do that for a living was incredibly appealing, although very much out of reach in terms of my ability, but it was a dream.

Alex Lorestani, CEO and co-founder, Geltor (Episode 185)

Maybe I was a little bit of an unusual twelve-year-old. But something that I've been very excited about from a young age was one day running a hospital where no one got sick there. I thought it was really weird that people would go to the hospital and get sicker from something that happened to them there. And that's what eventually led me on this path to go to medical school, graduate school, and eventually to start Geltor.

FACING THE SEDUCTION OF SUCCESS

Joan Sutton, CEO and founding partner, 707 Flora (Episode 189)

> I always wanted to be a veterinarian because I love animals. And then I quickly realized that as a veterinarian, you see sick animals, and I'm so sensitive, and it would always break my heart. . . . So I decided that wasn't the journey for me.

Robyn Watkins, founder and chief product developer, Holistic Beauty Group (Episode 191)

> Back then, I wanted to be a makeup artist. I was doing makeovers on all my friends. Growing up, my mother sold Avon, so I had all the makeup, I had all the products, and people would be lined up in my bathroom to get their makeup done, their hair done, a bubble bath, whatever. I was just doing all the beauty stuff.

MY BEGINNING

At age eleven, I wanted to be an archaeologist. Ancient Egyptian history had always been my favorite subject in school. I was riveted by the artifacts I saw in museums, and had an intense curiosity about ancient civilizations and faraway lands. I saw archaeology as fascinating and fun detective work, the living using forensic techniques to unearth clues and piece together knowledge about those who preceded them. Archeology felt full of adventure and romance. I can't pinpoint the moment when I turned away from that particular dream. However, I still have that curiosity, that desire to investigate worlds other than my own, that love of learning about people outside of my own little circle, and that passion for digging deeper to discover what's hidden beneath all the layers. In a way, that's the essence of *Where Brains Meet Beauty*. ❖

Lesson Learned

Keep your backpack open and keep filling it with skills, experiences, and dreams. You never know when its contents will come in handy on the unmapped journey ahead, at age eleven—or any age at all. ❖

SOUND BITE

Dream big because, why not?

FOOD FOR THOUGHT

➤ What career did your eleven-year-old self dream about?

➤ When and how did that dream change?

➤ What are the most significant lessons from your childhood or from your early years that are serving you well as an adult?

11

SKIN IN THE GAME

Typically, the final chapter in a book such as this one is devoted to a recap of what has come before, with wise observations, conclusions, and answers to the previously posed dilemmas, all neatly tied up in a bow. While I am as much a fan of neat bows as the next person, I cannot claim to have the answers that you might be expecting. Sorry to disappoint, but I have not (yet) mastered managing the seduction/success challenge. Sometimes I still get seduced by success—both the success I have achieved and the promise of greater success to come (mostly the latter). As mentioned, often that seduction is exciting, fun, and joyful. After all, if the road to success was only a negative experience, it would be much easier to find an exit ramp, reject the seduction and the success altogether, and go find some undemanding, albeit uninspiring, employment.

Yet even though I have not perfected (there's that word again!) the art of balance, I am now much better at dealing with the success siren's call. I have traversed enough speed bumps—including a global pandemic that derailed much of my industry—to feel reasonably confident that I can weather whatever storms are ahead. That confidence has liberated me from my earlier thinking that if I didn't put in those extra hours and spend every waking minute thinking about my enterprise, my business would never succeed.

So while I can't offer a universal secret sauce, I can summarize a few things in *my* secret sauce. Sometimes it's tastier than others, but it always adds flavor to my day. And it might contain a couple of ingredients that resonate with you. These are some of the truths I have learned about my business, my industry, and myself through speaking with my amazing *Where Brains Meet Beauty* guests during over two hundred conversations that highlighted every kind of business and personal hurdle—hurdles that tested commitment and character. These thoughts are not intended to be preachy or self-righteous. They're just my rules of the road, reminders of stuff you probably know in your heart but might have forgotten—things I have learned along the way to wherever I am.

Truth #1: Your road is *your* road. Each guest has a unique approach to seduction, success, and balancing the two. And since everyone charts their road to success a little differently, it's crucial to resist the temptation, promulgated by our social-media-centric world, to compare my approach or your approach to anyone else's. You learn a lot by listening to those around you, but it's also super important to filter out the negative stuff, and whatever just doesn't feel right for you. Thoughtful criticism can be valuable, but everyone has an opinion about everything, and not all of them are relevant or helpful. Separate the noise from the wisdom. The most important voice to listen to is your own.

Truth #2: Sharing is not just welcome; it's essential. While your road, your navigation style, and your final destination are uniquely yours, you will probably encounter some other travelers along the way. There are tasks, milestones, and goals in any industry that everyone must reach. In beauty and wellness, if you have an idea for a makeup, skincare, or supplement line, you need a formula, some evidence that it works, a package, a marketing strategy, a way to analyze results, and of course, financing. If you are offering a service, you need a place to provide it, and a trained team to deliver it, and of course, financing.

Within these basic requirements, there are a thousand differentiating details, but everyone has to create a general structure and plan before filling in all the blanks. That creates a commonality that can be comforting when shared. It can be reassuring to learn that you're not the only one who lies awake at night wondering how the new product launch will go. That worry is not a referendum on how you are doing as a business leader. Listening to my guests describe how they have handled all these details, I've learned about their everyday struggles, some of which I have experienced myself. While the focus of the podcast is on individual journeys, one of the purposes of bringing together my guests' experiences in this book is to show Guest A that Guest B had an interesting way of dealing with Common Challenge #17 that might be helpful.

Truth #3: We all need someone to lean on. Within any industry, professionals don't often get asked about their backstories or the stress, fears, and doubts they might be feeling as they build their business or climb the corporate ladder. When talking about your business to the press or on your website or blog, you may feel pressure to project cheer and optimism, always showing the marketplace that your product is superb, and everything is just great. You might (correctly) assess that your customers don't want to hear about the shipment that arrived late or the payroll you're struggling to meet. Yet everyone needs a way to vent, and an understanding shoulder to cry on. I have been that shoulder for my guests, and they have been that shoulder for me. I am not a reporter or a biographer. I am not a business advisor or a coach. I am just a colleague who wants to share my experience while my guests share theirs. This book is a storybook, not a workbook.

Truth #4: Remember where you started. And why. When I started Base Beauty, the agency that produces *Where Brains Meet*

Beauty, I did so with a sense of purpose. Of course, I wanted to lead an agency that made outstanding creative work for beauty and wellness industry clients. But the "why" and the "how" have always been as important to me as the "what." My overarching goal was to build a work environment that reflected my values, and a culture in which those with similar values would flourish. Early on, I laid out these values. And I am proud to say we have followed them rigorously. Now they are part of our DNA, reflected in every team member we hire, every client we choose to work with, and how we work together. These values are mentioned again and again in the stories presented here, and in the complete podcasts from which they have been synopsized. I have found that by letting them guide our work, Base Beauty has blossomed into an agency I am proud to lead—and one that reflects the values with which I try to live my life. Easy to list, harder to implement, at Base Beauty, we often remind each other of these core values:

- Respect, kindness, and empathy
- Pride in our work, ourselves, and each other
- Openness to differing opinions
- Diversity and inclusion
- Sustainability
- Peer-to-peer mentorship
- Philanthropy

Truth #5: Your team is as important as your clients, maybe more so. Practicing what we preach, these core values are integral to why we have such an outstanding, and I believe, unique team. As the agency began to grow—from our original little group who could all fit in an elevator to today's team of twenty-five, with departments and supervisors and organizational layers—I was determined to stay focused on my master plan and resist falling prey to the seduction of the company's increasing complexity. Early on, I realized that my team and the culture we created would be the key to all of it.

By respecting my team and encouraging them to respect each other, we have continued to experience that same delight and joy of camaraderie that we felt at the very beginning when we were carving out our niche and defining what we wanted to be. So we celebrate birthdays and holidays. We let people take time for doctor's appointments and school plays. We have each other's backs on good days and bad days, cheering our triumphs together and soothing our bumps and bruises together. As we emerged from the isolation of COVID-19, we started a Mental Health Day program, "requiring" that everyone take one mental health day a month to chill, recharge, eat junk food, sleep in, do a lot, or do nothing. No surprise that this is wildly popular, greatly appreciated, and has had an immediate impact on stress levels. By supporting each other in these ways, we end up producing great work for and lasting relationships with our clients.

The benefits of this approach are proven in the loyalty of team members—some of them have been with me from the very beginning—and the pleasure we experience in working hard together. Our clients often tell us that we are really fun to work with. Everyone feels valued. There's no better feeling than that.

So these are my truths, evolved (and still evolving) over four-plus decades of living, two-plus decades of working, and fifteen years of entrepreneur-ing. I hope there are nuggets here that are helpful to those in beauty and wellness and in other arenas. The challenges of leadership are universal.

If you've been intrigued or moved by any of the stories presented, I invite you to listen to or read our complete podcast episodes and dive more deeply into what makes each guest, their work, and their contributions to their industry at once extraordinary and wonderfully ordinary. Every conversation is fascinating. *Where Brains Meet Beauty* is a gathering of ambitious, smart, and scrappy souls who decided to follow their bliss and continue to work at it every single day. I am proud that we are part of the same industry.

My goal for myself is to be a perpetual work-in-progress, as a leader and as a person. I try to learn something every day. And I never forget to ring the bell of gratitude.

Wherever you and your business are headed, I wish you an inspiring journey, grace in managing the seduction, and success that fills you with joy. ✤

WISDOM IN THREE WORDS

Inspired by
Where Brains Meet Beauty

Suitable for bumper stickers, fridge magnets, cross-stitched samplers, or tee shirts, here are tiny phrases to glance at when you're stuck, frustrated, exhausted, or just having one of those days. Use them as inspiration or helpful reminders of stuff you already know.

Celebrate the joy

Do your homework

Find the fun

Always think strategically

Structure is freedom

Zig and zag

Learn to delegate

Remember the passion

Ask for help

Pay it forward

Perfection doesn't exist

Control doesn't exist

Balance doesn't exist

Mentor young talent

Share the burdens

Harness your power

Keep your perspective

Use the fear

Appreciate speed bumps

Do that tomorrow

Welcome new opportunities

"No" is okay

Listen to everyone

Ignore the naysayers

Always be you

Keep your dream

Tweak your dream

Seek the balance

Learn to juggle

Use your calendar

Stuff can wait

Pressure can kill

Always have compassion

People come first

Take the risk

Handshakes are powerful

Failure is scary

Success is scarier

Solutions aren't instant

Remember to breathe

We win together

Face the fear

Feel the feeling

Trust your team

Keep your focus

It'll get done

Learn from mistakes

Struggle isn't failure

Transparency is essential

Hire smart people

Listen to them

Make eye contact

Fear is motivating

Escape social media

Learn to pivot

Authenticity always wins

Bad days end

Never stop networking

Hire a mom

Always dig deeper

Learn every day

THE
BASE BEAUTY
STORY

eadquartered in New York City, Base Beauty Creative Agency (BBCA), producers of the podcast *Where Brains Meet Beauty,* is a full-service creative agency specializing in the beauty and wellness industries. We accelerate growth for our clients across all sales channels and marketing touchpoints. During fifteen years, the agency has built a reputation for expertise in creative and marketing for the beauty and wellness industries—planning and executing innovative strategies, designing eye-catching packaging, placing click-worthy social media messaging—for an impressive roster of consumer and professional brands. We launch brands from the ground up, we revive brands that need to refresh and recharge their look and their outreach, and we grow brands of all sizes, shapes, styles, and stages. Working thoughtfully and artfully, we keep pace with—and often set the pace for—what's going on in our fast-moving, fast-growing industry. Every day, we demonstrate that a fully integrated approach to marketing really works as we break down client silos to craft needle-moving marketing.

Along with our creative and marketing services, we share our knowledge and experience with the industry through our Master Class Presentation series and C-Suite Marketing Workshops. Members of our accomplished leadership team are often quoted in business publications, including *Glossy, WWD, Business of Fashion, The Washington Post,* and *Luxury Daily.* They are also featured at industry events, including Cosmoprof NA, ADF & PCD, Indie Beauty Expo, and Beauty Connect Summit.

Base Beauty is a WBENC-Certified Women's Business Enterprise, a recipient of the Enterprising Women of the Year Award, a recipient of the Best of Small Business Award, an A'Design 2021 Award Winner, a PAC IOU 2022 Award Winner, and a 2021 DesignRush accredited agency. The agency was selected as a finalist for the 2021 *Glossy* Worklife Awards in the category of Most Committed to Employee Appreciation.

Base Beauty welcomes inquiries from beauty, wellness, and personal care brands in high-growth mode. To see our work, services, and client list, visit basebeauty.com, and reach out to jodi@basebeauty.com. Also follow us on Instagram @BaseBeautyCreativeAgency, and "Jodi Katz" on LinkedIn. ❖

Where Brains Meet Beauty

In 2017, Base Beauty launched the podcast series *Where Brains Meet Beauty*. Hosted by BBCA founder and Creative Director Jodi Katz, the series invites beauty and wellness executives and entrepreneurs to share their wisdom and personal journeys, with the goal of humanizing the industry. Pre-pandemic, *Where Brains Meet Beauty* established a unique Podcast-in-Residence program with Saks Fifth Avenue at Saks' flagship store in New York City, offering live podcasting events and networking opportunities. *Where Brains Meet Beauty* is also a partner with the Beauty Connect Summit. The series is consistently ranked in the Top 5 iTunes podcasts in the Fashion/Beauty category. The stories presented here are synopsized from over two hundred podcast episodes.

For updates on *Where Brains Meet Beauty*, please follow us on Instagram (@wherebrainsmeetbeautypodcast). To listen to or read transcripts of complete podcast episodes, please visit @wherebrainsmeetbeautypodcast and search by guest name or episode number. ❖

MEET OUR GUESTS

Since launching in January of 2017, *Where Brain Meet Beauty* has hosted over two hundred guests, each with a remarkable story to tell. Other than a COVID-19 hiatus in the spring of 2020, we have continued to launch new episodes several times a month. Here's a complete roster of our guests up to the publication date, each with a little nugget from our conversation. Titles and affiliations noted are based on where each guest was at the time their episode was recorded. Some have since moved on and up.

We are still going strong! For new episodes, or to listen to or read transcripts of the complete episodes listed here, please visit wherebrainsmeetbeauty.com. For updates on the series, please follow us on Instagram @wherebrainsmeetbeautypodcast, or "Jodi Katz" on LinkedIn.

EPISODE 1

"Can this be recycled? Where is the waste going? How can we make this eco more clean, better for the world, and better for our customer?"
Ashley Prange, founder & CEO, Au Naturale Cosmetics

EPISODE 2

"Where I have had to exercise the most patience is in not being distracted by all the shiny objects in the beauty industry."
Brenda Brock, founder & formulator, Farmaesthetics

EPISODE 3

"I don't really fit in anywhere."
Jillian Wright, co-founder, Indie Beauty Media Group

EPISODE 4

"You need to be your own biggest cheerleader."
Jeannine Morris, multimedia journalist

EPISODE 5

"If I told people what I was doing, they would try to talk me out of it."
Wendi Berger, president & creator, Pour le Monde Parfums

EPISODE 6

"What do we have to say? Why should anyone listen to us?"
Samantha Citro, director of marketing & operations, Immunocologie

EPISODE 7

"The most successful people are open to helping other people."
Natalie Mackey, founder & CEO, Winky Lux

EPISODE 8

"How you treat others and how you treat yourself are the most important parts of work."
Jennifer Walsh, consultant & founder, Pride and Glory

EPISODE 9

"I'm a good corporate girl; I don't go anywhere without a deck!"
Elana Drell Szyfer, CEO, Laura Geller

EPISODE 10

"Our first job was producing a shoot for Madonna, and I thought I was going to die."
Tracy Murphy, founder, Lash Star

EPISODE 11

"There's nobody who doesn't second-guess themselves on a daily basis."
Ian Ginsberg, president, C.O. Bigelow Apothecaries

EPISODE 12

"Pressure creates diamonds."
Craig Dubitsky, founder, Hello Products

EPISODE 13

"It's all trial and error."
Jasmine Garnsworthy, founder, The Buff

EPISODE 14

"Set boundaries for yourself, respect your personal time."
Paulette Heller, vice president of marketing, Conair

EPISODE 15

"One of the keys to success is always saying yes."
Nick Arrojo, founder & owner, Arrojo

EPISODE 16

"The harder and more painful something is, the more I laugh about it."
Jennifer Kapahi, co-founder, trèStiQue

EPISODE 17

"Know your worth."
Tara Tersigni, COO, Beauty Evolution

EPISODE 18

"Carve out non-negotiable me-time for yourself."
Angela Kim, founder, Savor Beauty

EPISODE 19

"It's not all about hard work; it's about working intelligently."
Danielle Vincent, founder, Kimiko Beauty

EPISODE 20

"I love beauty. I love showing women a way to feel good about themselves."
Elisa Vitale, vice president of design, Base Beauty Creative Agency

EPISODE 21

"The law of reciprocity says that the more that we are in an energy of giving, the more that we'll find ourselves in the energy of receiving."
Alan Cohen, executive coach, Base Beauty Creative Agency

EPISODE 22

"Having brains and beauty is the ultimate combination; you're a force to be reckoned with."
Aleni Mackarey, COO, vice president of program success, Base Beauty Creative Agency

EPISODE 23

"The messaging always has to be very tactful, fresh, and new, because consumers are smarter than they ever were in the past."
Cate Charney, publicist, Base Beauty Creative Agency

EPISODE 24

"You have to move and try something else and get new experiences."
Andrea Halpern, publicist, Base Beauty Creative Agency

EPISODE 25

"Writing a tagline is about capturing the essence of a brand in four or five words. Each word has to pull its weight many times over."
Jan Michell, copywriter, Base Beauty Creative Agency

EPISODE 26

"Taking a sabbatical is a skill."
Justine Lackey, finance director, Base Beauty Creative Agency

EPISODE 27

"Ideas can come from anywhere."
Julie Chen, copywriter, Base Beauty Creative Agency

EPISODE 28

"People have lots of side hustles now."
Jessica Matlin, co-host, Fat Mascara

EPISODE 28

"If the to-do list isn't working, and I'm not getting stuff done, I'll set alarms."
Jenn Goldstein, co-host, Fat Mascara

EPISODE 29

"I learned long ago to leave my ego at home."
Maggie Ciafardini, beauty consultant

EPISODE 30

"It takes confidence to be generous."
Jane Park, CEO & founder, Julep

EPISODE 31

"Try to go back to the attitude of gratitude."
Tiffany Andersen, CEO, Tiffany Andersen Brands

EPISODE 32

"Private equity is about finding the right partner who can help you grow your business and take it to the next level."
Annette Rodriguez, managing director, Warburg Pincus

EPISODE 33

"Optimism goes a long way."
Lisa Devo & Shannon Burch, founders, Soap & Paper

EPISODE 34

"If you don't take a risk, you may not succeed."
Laurent Saffre, CEO, Pierre Fabre USA

EPISODE 35

"I just started saying 'yes.'"
Tim Quinn, vice president, creative artistry of Armani Beauty, L'Oreal

EPISODE 36

"You might have nine misses, but the tenth time, you hopefully have a hit."
Linda Mason, makeup artist

EPISODE 37

"It's better to get down and dirty and actually understand what's going on."
Evelyn Wang, senior vice president marketing, Wet N Wild

EPISODE 38

"I'm learning to love being a 'misfit.'"
Deanna Utroske, editor, CosmeticsDesign.com

EPISODE 39

"Beauty is such a universal language. It doesn't have any boundaries."
Ewelina Aiossa, assistant vice president of marketing, SkinCeuticals

EPISODE 40

"Use less. Love more."
Jeannie Jarnot, founder, Beauty Heroes

EPISODE 41

"I don't get overwhelmed. I've been doing this a long time, and I'm not young—
I have a little more patience."
Gay Timmons, founder, Oh, Oh Organic

EPISODE 42

"I really believe in living my craft."
Jessica Hanson, president & general manager, AmorePacific US

EPISODE 43

"Overall, you have to not take things personally in business."
Elizabeth Scherle, co-founder & president, Influenster

EPISODE 44

"I never want to put someone down for trying something—unless it's dangerous!"
Janell Hickman, beauty editor, BET

EPISODE 45

"Create a vision for yourself. Then trust in it."
Daniel Kaner, co-founder, Oribe Hair Care

EPISODE 46

"You don't get great things to happen by being mean, yelling, or throwing things."
Amanda Baldwin, president, Supergoop!

EPISODE 47

"I've followed a winding path to something that looks like a career."
Matthew Stillman, founder, Primal Derma

EPISODE 48

"Dance teaches you an incredible amount of discipline and professionalism."
Carey Channing, project coordinator, Base Beauty Creative Agency

EPISODE 49

"I don't believe in coincidence. I believe in synchronicities."
Joseph Quartana, founder/director, Parfums Quartana

EPISODE 50

"You can write a hundred emails. You might only get two responses. But who knows where those two responses will take you?"
Amanda Thesen, makeup artist

EPISODE 51

"I'm looking to improve what I currently have, instead of coming up with the next big thing every six months."
Marisa Arredondo, founder & CEO, Phace Bioactive

EPISODE 52

"No one's going to come knocking on your door; you've got to get out."
Margarita Arriagada, chief merchant, Sephora

EPISODE 53

"Networking is more about putting a hand out than taking a hand."
Caroline Fabrigas, CEO, Scent Marketing Inc.

EPISODE 54

"Your feelings, emotions, and opinions all matter because you matter."
Cassandra Bankson, online beauty pioneer & influencer

EPISODE 55

"Work on your messaging and reshuffle the content until you see progress in your storytelling."
Paul Peros, CEO, Foreo

EPISODE 56

"A good designer can design around the constraints and still make something beautiful."
Laszlo Moharita, global director of beauty products, Johnson & Johnson

EPISODE 57

"You can dream big, but start strategically and don't try to grow too fast."
Stacey Levine, co-founder, Glo Science

EPISODE 58

"You can tell the difference between someone who's completely prepared and someone who's winging it."
Laura Gerchik, general manager, Biologique Recherche USA

EPISODE 59

"I thought I was doing fine, but I learned that I was not."
Erin Williams, owner, Erin's Face

EPISODE 60

"Intuition is such an understated thing in this world."
Angela Irish, president & co-founder, OZNaturals

EPISODE 61

"Bring other people in. You don't have to be the goddess of 'I know everything.'"
Marcia Kilgore, founder, Beauty Pie, Bliss Spa, Soap & Glory, FitFlop

EPISODE 62

"What are you interested in? That's what you need to walk toward."
Lauren Katz, senior creative strategist, Mororccanoil

EPISODE 63

"I believed in what I had, so I just went forward."
Nannette de Gaspé Beaubien, founder, Nannette de Gaspé

EPISODE 64

"Try to get away from top-down structure and really uplift and listen to the young entry-level individuals."
Daniela Ciocan, marketing director, Cosmoprof North America

EPISODE 65

"I didn't have any skincare routine—I learned it all in Korea."
Charlotte Cho, founder, Soko Glam

EPISODE 66

"The human touch is really what it's all about."
Kristy Engels, senior vice president, Beauty Strategy Group and Beauty Barrage

EPISODE 67

"If I was a TV character, I'd be Brenda Walsh, 90210."
Francesco Clark, founder, Clark's Botanicals

EPISODE 68

"When you're building a company, look ahead and imagine what the company should be if you're the market leader."
Mariya Nurislamova, CEO & co-founder, Scentbird/Deck of Scarlet

EPISODE 69

"There's no such thing as a great entrepreneur who didn't ride some great wave."
Barry Beck, co-founder & COO, Bluemercury

EPISODE 70

"We want people to have a better, more intuitive experience."
Leigh Adelman, co-founder, Artis

EPISODE 70

"Just see this idea from the wire to wind; just make it happen."
Jeremy Adelman, co-founder, Artis

EPISODE 71

"What could be more inspiring than helping the next generation of entrepreneurs?"
Alicia Sontag, co-founder, Prelude Growth Partners

EPISODE 71

"It's all about the human connection."
Carla Ruiz, vice president, business development, Johnson & Johnson

EPISODE 72

"As women, we need to band together and lift each other up."
Elise Saetta, fashion beauty director, Macy's

EPISODE 73

"You can be a great CEO, a great mother, and a great wife/partner, but you can't be all three in the same day."
Dawn Robertson, founder, Timeless Beauty Bar

EPISODE 74

"Making other people grow, whether that's professionally or personally, that's what I define as success."
Mabel Lee, founder, Velour Lashes

EPISODE 75

"If you're having a bad day. . .just pretend you're Madonna or Beyonce. Act like a queen."
Gina Way, beauty writer & expert

EPISODE 76

"Be a problem solver, not a people pleaser."
Cathi Singh, makeup artist and owner, LemonPenny

EPISODE 77

"Listen to someone who has a completely different experience than yours."
Rachel Winard, founder, Soapwalla

EPISODE 78

"There are some people who work very hard, and some who work very smart."
Divya Gugnani, CEO & founder, Wander Beauty

EPISODE 79

"*Perfect* is such a confusing word because often it has been created by other people's expectations."
Poppy Jamie, founder, Happy Not Perfect

EPISODE 80

"When you're open to things, they come."
Kelly Campbell, agency growth consultant & host, Thrive Podcast

EPISODE 81

"In the beginning, was I the best colorist? No. Did I do my best? Definitely."
Kim Vo, celebrity colorist & entrepreneur

EPISODE 82

"Be respectful. But speak up."
Danya Klein, vice president, brand relations, Preen.Me

EPISODE 83

"Being vulnerable is incredibly powerful."
Giorgos Tsetis, co-founder & CEO, Nutrafol

EPISODE 84

"It's possible to run companies in ways that are nurturing, guiding, transformative."
Kathy Van Ness, COO, Golden Door Properties

EPISODE 85

"It's always about the client."
Delon Nelson, founder, D&I Fitness

EPISODE 86

"I can't tell my daughter to go after her dreams if I'm not willing to do the same myself."
Alexandra Bradberry, co-founder, The Sparkle Bar

EPISODE 87

"I lived through it. I handled it. It doesn't scare me anymore."
Lisa Price, founder, Carol's Daughter

EPISODE 88

"I had no hairstylists, no insurance, no brand, no biz. I just wanted someone to do my hair."
Erika Wasser, founder, Glam & Go

EPISODE 89

"You can't keep what you don't give away."
Brian "Gibs" Long, founder & CEO, GIBS Grooming

EPISODE 90

"Failure is not scary. Success is scary. Prepare for success."
Tye Caldwell, co-founder, ShearShare

EPISODE 90

"Great ideas start on the inside."
Courtney Caldwell, co-founder, ShearShare

EPISODE 91

"I try not to get too attached to things. Inevitably, you lose them."
Lisa Goodman, founder, GoodSkin Clinics

EPISODE 92

"What you repeat, you strengthen."
Taryn Toomey, founder & CEO, The Class

EPISODE 93

"I'm a big believer in the fallacy of multitasking."
Michael Marquis, president, Vogue International

EPISODE 94

"Is it madness or entrepreneurship?"
Sue Ismiel, founder & global beauty ambassador, Nad's

EPISODE 95

"Just put a little blush on; you'll feel better!"
Kimberly Soane, executive director, Bobbi Brown

EPISODE 96

"What's more engaging than sex?"
Rachel Braun Sherl, managing partner & co-founder, SPARK Solutions for Growth

EPISODE 97

"You always have to know that you don't know everything."
Andrea Bifulco, founder, Nose University

EPISODE 98

"The first ten years were not easy."
Laura Slatkin, founder & executive chairman, NEST Fragrances

EPISODE 99

"I just really enjoy doing hair and making people feel good about themselves."
Eloise Cheung, editorial & celebrity hairstylist

EPISODE 100

"More than anything, I think it's important to be curious."
Trish McEvoy, founder, Trish McEvoy Beauty

EPISODE 101

"That's how things work, right? Somebody just out of the blue pops up, and all of a sudden your prayers are answered."
Beth Russell, founder, House of Potentia

EPISODE 102

"If your team needs you that badly, then you don't have a very good team."
Rita Hazan, celebrity colorist & owner, Rita Hazan Salon

EPISODE 103

"If your motivation is only money, you're going to wear out pretty quickly."
Blair James, owner & co-founder, Bondi Sands

EPISODE 104

"Failure just hasn't been an option for me."
Rachel Roff, founder, Urban Skin Rx

EPISODE 105

"I get a lot of energy figuring out how to make an impact."
Nancy McKay, CEO, Barefoot Scientist

EPISODE 106

"A lot of life is just showing up."
Tina Hedges, founder, LOLI Beauty

EPISODE 107

"Working with my mom has given me a lot of confidence."
Rachel Piskin, co-founder, ChaiseFitness

EPISODE 107

"My daughter grew my business in a way I couldn't have."
Lauren Piskin, co-founder, ChaiseFitness

EPISODE 108

"Tell yourself you're worthy and you belong. You'll eventually believe it."
Essence Gant, beauty director, BuzzFeed

EPISODE 109

"Don't let 'urgent' get in the way of 'important.'"
Georgina Gooley, co-founder, Billie

EPISODE 110

"I define myself by what I do."
Camille McDonald, advisor & brand consultant

EPISODE 111

"Don't rush it; do what you want."
Dr. Patricia Wexler, cosmetic dermatologist

EPISODE 112

"In high school, I wanted to make my own way in the world, and I wanted to own a pink Lamborghini."
Rochelle Weitzner, CEO & founder, Pause Well-Aging

EPISODE 113

"I only want to be around people with good energy."
Alison Engstrom, founder & editor-in-chief, ROSE & IVY Journal

EPISODE 114

"If you don't ask, you won't get what you're looking for."
Maura Cannon Dick, CMO, FitSkin

EPISODE 115

"At the end of the day, you need to be the one who forges your own path."
Asha Coco, vice president of sales & business development, Givaudan

EPISODE 116

"The thing that's been missing in oral care is the power of the smile."
Julian and Cody Levine, co-founders, Twice

EPISODE 117

"Smell really drives a lot of what we do."
Erika Shumate, co-founder & CEO, Pinrose Perfume

EPISODE 118

"We're little, but we're mighty."
Amy Shecter, CEO, Glamsquad

EPISODE 119

"Beauty is really about embracing what you love about yourself."
Jane Larkworthy, brand consultant, beauty editor-at-large, The Cut

EPISODE 120

"I don't care how great your algorithm is; there needs to be a human factor, too."
Kristen Wiley, CEO & founder, Statusphere

EPISODE 121

"This platform is going to change the beauty industry."
Jacqueline Gutierrez, founder, Beauty Backer

EPISODE 122

"I was at a rock and a hard place. I couldn't take pills, and I couldn't not take pills. . . . I knew that something had to give."
Dr. Gregory Brown, founder, RéVive Skincare

EPISODE 123

"You have to have compassion for everybody around you."
Elise Joy, executive director, Girls Helping Girls. Period.

EPISODE 124

"I love fancy. I always did."
Eric Buterbaugh, founder, Eric Buterbaugh Fragrances

EPISODE 125

"Any successful businessperson will tell you that failure is an inevitable part of that path."
Julie Wald, founder, CEO, & chief wellness officer, Namaste New York

EPISODE 126

"I'm loyal to brands. I'm loyal to formulas."
Bart Kaczanowicz, founder, OMGBART.com

EPISODE 127

"Don't try to control everything."
Sue Nabi, CEO, Coty

EPISODE 128

"We were just two girls from Queens."
Gabrielle Ophals, co-founder, Haven Spa

EPISODE 129

"I hit the kitchen and started mixing stuff up myself."
Heather Reier, founder & CEO, Cake Beauty

EPISODE 130

"There are so many brands out there with such potential."
Allison Slater Ray, president, Memebox

EPISODE 131

"My move to California was a clear sign that my life was supposed to take a dramatic turn."
Cheryl Foland, founder & CEO, lilah b.

EPISODE 132

"Failure is so underrated. What a huge gift it is."
Jessica Johnson, founder & CEO, Jessica Johnson Beauty

EPISODE 133

"Victorialand Beauty is fun. It's happiness. It's acceptance. It's no judgment."
Victoria Watts, founder, Victorialand Beauty

EPISODE 134

"Selling a business to investors is sort of like speed dating."
John Costanza, CEO, Beauty Quest Group

EPISODE 135

"Just send the email. What have you got to lose?"
Kirsten Kjaer Weis, founder, Kjaer Weis

EPISODE 136

"The nice thing about running a small business is that we get to create the policies we want."
Laura Schubert, CEO & co-founder, Fur

EPISODE 137

"Weight management is not a sprint; it's a marathon."
Tanya Zuckerbrot, CEO & founder, F-Factor

EPISODE 138

"I was kind of missing something in my life—I wanted to get challenged again."
Dr. Marc Ronert, owner & founder, Hush & Hush

EPISODE 139

"Stay focused on the dream you have for your business."
Rea Ann Silva, founder & CEO, Beautyblender

EPISODE 140

"I'm an interpreneur, finding great partners and great resources within these companies to test and learn."
Stephanie Kramer, SVP global marketing & product innovation, SkinCeuticals

EPISODE 141

"I thought I could crush it at multitasking. It actually isn't that productive."
Emily Culp, CEO, Cover FX

EPISODE 142

"It's as much a passion about the makeup as it is about cultivating and mentoring other women."
Wende Zomnir, founding partner, Urban Decay Cosmetics

EPISODE 143

"It was about more than creating an eye cream. It was about creating this community."
Sarah Kugelman, CEO and founder, skyn ICELAND

EPISODE 144

"My 'aha' moment was realizing people can do this for a living."
Amy Carra, senior director of brand innovation, Universal Beauty Products, Inc.

EPISODE 145

"I think every day, we're trying to balance."
Sasha Plavsic, founder, ILIA Beauty

EPISODE 146

"If you believe it, you can do it."
Deborah Lippmann, celebrity manicurist & founder, Deborah Lippmann

EPISODE 147

"Our parents lit this torch, and now it's our chance."
Inessa Vike, co-founder, Vike Beauty

EPISODE 147

"You never know where that connection could go. Just nurture that connection, relationship, and it could literally blossom."
Alina Vike, co-founder, Vike Beauty

EPISODE 148

"I'm performing every day. In the beauty world, you have to be on stage."
David Pirrotta, founder & CEO, David Pirrotta Brands

EPISODE 149

"For me, the worst thing is to be static and complacent."
Paige Novick, founder, Paige Novick Jewelry and Lifestyle

EPISODE 150

"We all thrive on community, now more than ever."
Natasha Cornstein, CEO, Blushington

EPISODE 151

"You are never too young and never too old to be who you always wanted to be."
Karissa Bodnar, founder & CEO, Thrive Causemetics

EPISODE 152

"The landscape is so cluttered. It gets confusing for consumers."
Diana Briceno, CEO, No B.S. Skincare

EPISODE 153

"The most important thing about a brand is developing an incredible relationship with your customer."
Frédéric Fekkai, founder & CEO, Fekkai

EPISODE 154

"Going silver is one of the most courageous things I've ever done, without even realizing it."
Manon Crespi, co-founder & CEO, Manon des Sources

EPISODE 155

"I want all women to be able to reach their full potential and feel beautiful."
Alicia Grande, founder & CEO, Grande Cosmetics

EPISODE 156

"Instead of being pessimistic, we said, 'What can we do that honors our mission?'"
Doreen Bloch, executive director, Makeup Museum

EPISODE 157

"Pay attention to opportunities that come up when you least expect them. Don't be afraid. Just go for it."
Dr. Ava Shamban, dermatologist & founder, AVA MD and SKIN FIVE Clinics

EPISODE 158

"To me, age is a number. There is nothing that a person can't do if they're still willing to learn and grow."
Joy Harari, founder & CEO, Shore Magic

EPISODE 159

"Just because something doesn't work, doesn't mean you're a failure."
Fiona Stiles, celebrity makeup artist, founder & creative director, Reed Clarke

EPISODE 160

"If you have your health, you have everything."
Dara Levy, founder, DERMAFLASH

EPISODE 161

"Brand is everything in beauty and skincare."
Steve Weigler, founder, EmergeCounsel

EPISODE 162

"Better a 'whoops' than a 'what if?'"
Gwen Jimmere, CEO & founder, Naturalicious

EPISODE 163

"Everyone was reading the *Financial Times,* and I was reading *Vogue.*"
Maria Hatzistefanis, founder, The Rodial Group

EPISODE 164

"When you have a family business, people put their heart and soul into it."
Sonya Dakar, founder, Sonya Dakar

EPISODE 165

"Dermatologists were very, very afraid to treat darker skin tones. So we met a whole host of needs."
Dr. Susan Taylor, founder, Skin of Color Society

EPISODE 166

"In the crazy lives we lead, we don't need more darkness. We need luminosity."
Veronique Gabai, founder & CEO, Veronique Gabai

EPISODE 167

"I felt like women of color were not well represented and could use a resource."
Pam Zapata, CEO, Society Eighteen

EPISODE 168

"It's SFSN. It sounds fabulous, it signifies nothing."
Jess Weiner, CEO & founder, Talk to Jess

EPISODE 169

"Your skin is your first and most lasting impression."
Dr. Michele Koo, founder & CEO, Dr. Koo Skincare

EPISODE 170

"I've always felt like the ultimate outsider."
Priya Rao, executive editor, Glossy & host, the Glossy Beauty Podcast

EPISODE 171

"Society told me that if you want to look your best, you have to straighten your hair."
Yve-Car Momperousse, founder & CEO, Kreyol Essence

EPISODE 172

"The energy of creation does not have to be chaos."
Anisa Telwar Kaicker, founder & CEO, Anisa International, Inc.

EPISODE 173

"Our big goal was to make the user experience amazing."
Lisa Ballstaedt, co-founder, Soon Skincare

EPISODE 173

"I've been in the world of finance and accounting for a long time. I was kind of bored of it."
Kayla Bertagna, co-founder, Soon Skincare

EPISODE 174

"I fantasized about meetings and powering myself with caffeine."
Ada Juristovski, co-founder, Nala

EPISODE 174

"It's really up to us to take up responsibility for our health and start caring for ourselves."
Mila Juristovski, co-founder, Nala

EPISODE 175

"I've had to take a moment for myself, because I can't pour from an empty cup."
Beatrice Dixon, co-founder & CEO, The Honey Pot Company

EPISODE 176

"Anticipation of what could go sideways creates the issue."
Casey Georgeson, CEO & founder, Saint Jane

EPISODE 177

"Calling it the beauty industry sounds like you are selling or creating beauty and packaging it up."
Dr. Zahir Dossa, CEO & co-founder, Function of Beauty

EPISODE 178

"Life is about turning lemons into lemonade, and the difficult times are when we learn the most."
Suzanne Somers, actress, author, & founder, Suzanne Organics

EPISODE 179

"We need to change the stigma of what cannabis is—it's not just THC."
Michael Bumgarner, founder, Cannuka

EPISODE 180

"It's not that I take on challenges and am not afraid—I take on challenges and act despite being afraid."
Soyoung Kang, chief marketing officer, eos Products

EPISODE 181

"I think transparency is what's being asked for. Radical transparency."
Indie Lee, founder & CEO, Indie Lee & Co.

EPISODE 182

"Quality has a price—I don't give myself any limit."
Kilian Hennessy, founder, Kilian Paris

EPISODE 183

"Innovation doesn't happen in your comfort zone."
Leslie Harris, global general manager, SkinCeuticals

EPISODE 184

"I don't want people to have to comb through ingredient lists."
Alissa Sasso, manager of consumer health, Environmental Defense Fund+Business

EPISODE 185

"We're running out of antibiotics to use."
Alex Lorestani, co-founder & CEO, Geltor Inc.

EPISODE 186

"Mostly everything can wait until the next business day."
Dana Jackson, founder & CEO, Beneath Your Mask

EPISODE 187

"Look for and celebrate the things that are going well. Even when things are mostly not going well."
Amy Gordinier, founder & CEO, SkinFix

EPISODE 188

"We're all motivated, hustling women—we'll figure it out."
Jenna Owens, founder, Fitish CBD Skincare

EPISODE 189

"The selling comes from my heart because I love it and want to share it."
Joan Sutton, CEO & founding partner, 707 Flora

EPISODE 190

"New luxury is all about a strong emotional connection, real community, and sustainability."
Sarah Willersdorf, managing director & partner, global head of luxury, Boston Consulting Group

EPISODE 191

"It's that old school 'believe in yourself' talk that can really take you far."
Robyn Watkins, founder & chief product developer, Holistic Beauty Group

EPISODE 192

"At the end of the day, there's room for all of us."
Emily Perez, Director of Safety, Regulatory Claims, Micro Acquisition, & Integration, L'Oreal, founder, Latinas in Beauty

EPISODE 193

"Sometimes doing things first is more valuable than thinking things through."
Sarah Lee, co-founder & co-CEO, Glow Recipe

EPISODE 193

"The path might be messy, and it might not be perfect, but we'll get there."
Christine Chang, co-founder & co-CEO, Glow Recipe

EPISODE 194

"How can we build a culture where all opinions are heard?"
Jeremy Soine, CEO, Face Reality

EPISODE 195

"Find your people. Your people are out there."
Sara Happ, founder & CEO, Sara Happ Inc.

EPISODE 196

"Nothing is perfect in this world; we need to learn to be flexible."
Evelyn Subramaniam, founder, BIJA ESSENCE

EPISODE 197

"With new leadership comes new direction."
Stephanie Morimoto, owner & CEO, Asutra

EPISODE 198

"I trusted my gut that I would figure it out."
Melissa Sperau, president of US, Shiseido Americas Corporation

EPISODE 199

"If you hire somebody to do something, you have to trust them to do it."
Samantha Bergmann, co-founder, HETIME

EPISODE 199

"At some point in their career, everybody should work in retail."
Christopher Carl, co-founder, HETIME

EPISODE 200

"I think the most important part about being a physician is the relationship you develop with your patients."
Dr. Muneeb Shah, influencer & dermatologist

EPISODE 201

"We should accept the fact that not getting an A every time means that the test was probably hard."
Nick Greenfield, co-founder, Candid

EPISODE 202

"If you could look at life with gratitude, then it's all upside."
Amy Errett, CEO & founder, Madison Reed

Many more episodes to come. Stay tuned!

ABOUT THE AUTHORS

Jodi Katz

Jodi Katz has been a respected voice in the beauty and wellness industry for almost twenty years, fifteen of them as founder and creative director of Base Beauty Creative Agency. Her career has spanned the quickly evolving communications marketplace. She started in advertising at the legendary agency BBDO, followed by positions on the editorial side of *Cosmopolitan* and *Glamour* magazines, then back to advertising at Mezzina/Brown. Next was work as a freelance copywriter for the Bliss and Avon beauty catalogs. Prior to launching Base Beauty, Jodi was a copywriter for the global prestige French brand L'Occitane en Provence, quickly climbing to creative director for the United States. Upon establishing Base Beauty, she took the bold step of positioning the agency as specialists in the beauty and wellness space, and has since built it into the go-to boutique agency for outstanding beauty creative solutions.

Jodi has been a featured speaker at many industry events, including Cosmoprof, Indie Beauty Expo, and Beauty Connect. She is the host of *Where Brains Meet Beauty,* the noted podcast produced by Base Beauty, with over two hundred episodes offering insightful conversations on the personal journeys of beauty and wellness industry leaders. She forged a longstanding partnership between *Where Brains Meet Beauty* and the Beauty Connect event series. Jodi has been featured in *WWD*, *Glossy*, and

Business of Fashion, and is a recipient of the Enterprising Women of the Year Award.

Jodi is a graduate of Lafayette College, with a degree in government in law.

She lives in New Jersey with her husband and two children. Her hobbies include fitness, Rent the Runway, and watching reality TV on Bravo. (Her current favorite show is *Below Deck*.)

Jan Michell

Jan Michell is a seasoned writer with over twenty-five years of experience creating compelling copy for an impressive clientele and a diverse array of projects. Her portfolio ranges from tiny startups to Fortune 500s, from fashion to food to pharma, and, of course, beauty, including web, print, branding, and packaging. She has worked with agencies, large and small, and directly with clients, large and small, launching new businesses and rebranding established ones. Her expertise revolves around taking complex, multi-tiered, or even murky information, diving deep, and turning it into cohesive, clear messaging that connects on both an intellectual and an emotional level. She is a passionate communicator, knowing how to grab her reader's attention and hold it, no matter what story she is telling.

A graduate of Skidmore College, Jan's writing journey began in the arts as a grant application writer and fundraiser for major and not-so-major dance companies. That's where she honed her powers of persuasion as she sought support for organizations she believed in. During her time in the dance world, she also wrote reviews and recommendations for dance companies applying for state funding. From there, she transitioned into direct marketing as a print catalog writer, then to advertising and e-commerce, and more recently, into website building and branding. She has been part of award-winning creative teams, including work on several Davey Award-winning projects. With *Facing the Seduction of Success*, she adds the title of author to her resume.

Jan lives in New York City with her husband. She has two grown children.

ACKNOWLEDGMENTS

Jodi Katz

Anyone who knows me at all—even if it's just through this book—knows that I believe in teams. In fact, building the right team is something I think I'm really good at—a talent I am lucky to possess since it contributes directly to my success, both personally and professionally. I am honored that so many extraordinary souls are on my team.

Here's to those who have been by my side on this journey that started five years ago with our first *Where Brains Meet Beauty* podcast guest, and is culminating in this meaningful storybook, with many more episodes and stories to come. Thanks to you all for lifting me up, cheering me up, and shaking me up along the way:

- My co-author, Jan Michell, who has a rare ability to take my thoughts and express them in words that are honestly and authentically mine. (Fun fact about Jan: it was her talented copywriting that created *Where Brains Meet Beauty* as our Base Beauty agency tagline, later usurped as the perfect name for our podcast.)
- Aleni Mackarey, who was there at the beginning of *Where Brains Meet Beauty* (and well before), and is still here, expertly nurturing it at every step.

- Carey Channing, the masterful producer of *Where Brains Meet Beauty* who, quite literally, made each episode happen.
- Esperanza Rosenbaum, producer (and so much more) of *Where Brains Meet Beauty* who helped in immeasurable ways to make sure our I's were dotted and our T's were crossed.
- Nico Osborne, our inspiring sound engineer who enables our stories to reach our listeners and smoothly navigates every technical speed bump.
- Alan Cohen, my wizard of a business coach, who came up with the brilliant idea that I start a podcast.
- Everyone at Base Beauty, a remarkable team dedicated to showing the world that work and leadership can be different, and that success can grow from a place of kindness, respect, and fun. They truly are where brains meet beauty!
- My husband, David, for being my biggest cheerleader, always believing in me, my ambition, and the business I am building.
- My kids, who I suspect secretly think it's cool that their mom has a podcast (but would never admit it).

Ring the bell!

To again quote the simple and wise words of one of our guests (see Chapter Seven), "No one does this alone." The "this" refers to the Herculean effort of starting and growing a business, but I submit it can be applied to any major endeavor, including writing a book.

So I would like to thank those who made sure I was not traveling this road alone:

- My co-author, Jodi Katz, for inviting me to join her on this extraordinary journey, and for countless opportunities over a decade of work together on projects that stretched me creatively in directions I could never have imagined.

- Our editor, Henry DeVries, for his always patient, always clear, and always helpful expertise and kindness to a first-time author.

- Carey Channing, producer extraordinaire of the *Where Brains Meet Beauty* podcast, for responding quickly and cheerfully to every request and sharing her intimate knowledge of our guests and their stories.

- Julie Chen, my erstwhile colleague at Base Beauty and collaborator on *Where Brains Meet Beauty* podcasts, who paved the way for my involvement in the series with sharp insights into those early episodes.

- Tickle Mhlambiso at Base Beauty, for meticulously pulling together details from over two hundred podcast episodes.

- The entire team at Indie Books International, for their thoughtful and generous support throughout.
- Aleni Mackarey, who keeps things humming at Base Beauty, who knows or finds the answer to every question in an instant, and who is always a sweet, smart cheerleader and invaluable problem solver.
- The entire Base Beauty team, because they are actually as extraordinary as described in these pages, offering constant support for every agency endeavor, including this book, whether they are directly involved or not.
- And finally, to my amazing husband for taking pride in my efforts, and for his endless patience as I wilted at the end of many long days.

My deepest thanks.

CPSIA information can be obtained
at www.ICGtesting.com
Printed in the USA
BVHW091429200522
637460BV00003B/6

9 781957 651101